Gazette Pall Mall

Royal Naval Exhibition - 1891

The Illustrated Handbook and Souvenir

Gazette Pall Mall

Royal Naval Exhibition - 1891
The Illustrated Handbook and Souvenir

ISBN/EAN: 9783337246525

Printed in Europe, USA, Canada, Australia, Japan

Cover: Foto ©ninafisch / pixelio.de

More available books at **www.hansebooks.com**

ROYAL NAVAL EXHIBITION

1891

The Illustrated Handbook and Souvenir.

Price Sixpence.

"PALL MALL GAZETTE" OFFICE, 2 NORTHUMBERLAND STREET, STRAND, LONDON W.C.

THE FIGHTING ON THE LAKE.

THE WORKING MODELS OF THE "MAJESTIC" (BARBETTE) AND THE "EDINBURGH" (TURRET) IN BATTLE; MAGAZINE ON BOARD THE "MAJESTIC" BLOWN UP; TORPEDO BOAT SUNK.

ROYAL NAVAL EXHIBITION:

Pall Mall Gazette "Extra." No. 56.

JUNE 1891. [*Price SIXPENCE.*

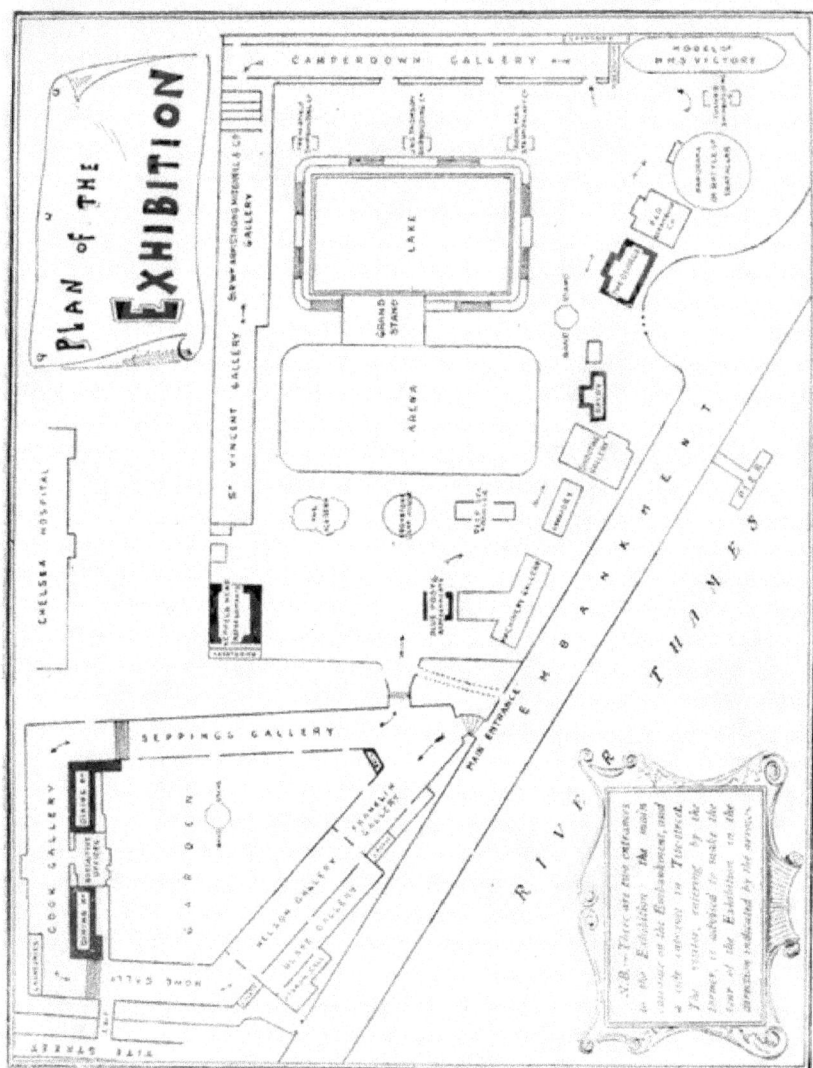

CONTENTS.

INTRODUCTION.

THE object of the present *Pall Mall* "Extra" is sufficiently explained by its title: "An Illustrated Handbook and Souvenir." Exhibition visitors may be divided into two classes. There are, first, the studious experts, proof against "exhibition headache," who will make a point of examining every exhibit, good, bad, and indifferent, and for whom nothing short of the exhaustive Official Catalogue will suffice. And, secondly, there is "the general visitor," who welcomes some assistance in selecting the most memorable and attractive exhibits only. It is for this kind of visitor that the following pages aim at supplying an illustrated guide and pictorial souvenir. The Plan of the Exhibition (on p. 3) will have sufficiently explained the method on which this Guide is arranged. The visitor who does not care to make the complete tour, but who wishes to consult the Guide on any particular section of the Exhibition, will at once find what he wants by consulting the table of contents given above.

We assume the visitor to enter by the main entrance on the Embankment. Over this entrance are inscribed the words (taken from the "Articles of War"), which set the key-note, as it were, to the Exhibition:—

> IT IS ON THE NAVY, UNDER THE GOOD PROVIDENCE OF GOD, THAT OUR WEALTH, PROSPERITY, AND PEACE DEPEND.

Facing the entrance is a trophy showing the arms, ancient and modern, by which "Britannia rules the waves." The visitor should, however, pause before proceeding, to note the instructive diagrams (on the wall to the right of the entrance) which Captain Sir J. Colomb, M.P., has prepared to illustrate the relation between Britannia's naval expenditure and naval responsibilities. The squares stand for the latter, measured by the extent of sea-commerce; the guns, for the former.

CHAPTER I.

THE FRANKLIN GALLERY.—ARCTIC RELICS, MODELS, &c.

Not here ! the white North has thy bones ; and thou,
    Heroic sailor-soul,
Art passing on thine happier voyage now
    Toward no earthly pole.

THE first section of the Naval Exhibition is devoted to what are known as the Franklin relics—to a collection of trophies from the region of thick-ribbed ice which surrounds the North Pole. Here is temporarily stored all that practically remains of the ill-fated exploring expedition which set out under the command of that "heroic sailor-soul," Sir John Franklin, in 1845. At the time mentioned Franklin had made his name famous by the discoveries of his land expeditions along the northern shores of America. When, therefore, it was thought expedient that a party should proceed to the icy seas of the far north, it was to him that the promoters of the exploration scheme naturally turned. Franklin, although 60 years of age, unhesitatingly accepted

IN THE TENT AT NIGHT.

command of two vessels—vessels whose names, like that of the *Victory*, are inscribed upon our naval annals in letters of gold—and with the *Erebus* and *Terror* set sail for the Arctic Ocean on May 19, 1845. Everybody expected great things. Franklin possessed both experience and skill ; he was known, moreover, to be a man of unquestionable courage and determination. His officers, again, were most carefully selected ; his sailors were men of discipline and of robust health : and his ships were fitted out with all that previous experience could suggest. Never did expedition start under more favourable auspices, and men's hopes ran high as they thought of the rich gains to science and to the art of navigation that it would inevit-

AN ARCTIC EXPEDITION ON THE MARCH.

ably bring back. But their hopes were vain—

The white North has his bones.

Nothing remains of the expedition which set out so gaily in 1845, and of the various Relief parties which succeeded it, but the scanty relics now temporarily housed in the Franklin Gallery of the Royal Exhibition at Chelsea. Nothing, did we say? Yes, there is something—something which, perhaps, after all is worth more than the glory of scientific discovery, more even than the winning of battles. There remains the imperishable record of the heroism and endurance of men who

. . . were English in heart and in limb,
Strong with the strength of the race to command, to
obey, to endure.

journeyed north—the whole accessible expanse of the ice-covered cap of the world was scrutinised with microscopic care, in the hope that here and there in the great silent waste there might be found some stray relic of the gallant fellows who had sailed away in the Northland and had never been seen again. Here—carefully preserved in glass cases—will be found bottles, anvil blocks, scraps of leather and wood, pieces of copper, salt-meat bones, charred wood, knife-blades, silver boxes, buttons, pencil-cases, rudder-irons, watches, medicine-cases—everything, in fact, which an abortive expedition of the kind might be likely to leave behind. Guns, books, prayer-books, and Christian melodies, the "Vicar of Wakefield," a small Bible interlined in many places, and a New Testament in French are also

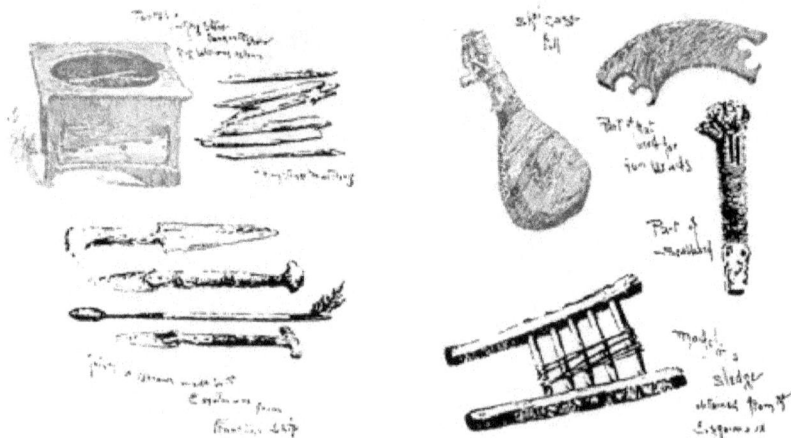

The Arctic Sub-division of the Navigation Section is one of the first things which will strike the visitor to the Naval Exhibition. It fronts the entrance and cannot possibly be missed. Foremost among the exhibits which it contains is a realistic representation of a hummocky ice-pack, along which four wax-work men laboriously drag a sledge, while a mariner awaits them at the door of the tent which they are about to occupy. The men are all rigged out with snow-goggles, cavernous mittens, and other articles of apparel essential to a locality where the thermometer is often 45 degrees below zero. Around this tableau are grouped the Franklin relics—objects which represent the tangible outcome of the various search expeditions which were sent out either to find the great explorer if alive or to discover his fate if dead. During the thirty years which followed 1848—the year in which the first search party

among the scanty gleanings of the great quest. These objects are all catalogued at length in the Official Guide—to which the student, as distinguished from the casual visitor, may be referred.

We may here notice another exhibit illustrative of life in the Arctic regions—an iceberg model, the interior of which is fitted up to represent the abandonment of the Investigator. The model stands in the grounds of the Exhibition, near the model of the Eddystone Lighthouse, and admission to the interior costs sixpence. The Investigator, under Captain McClure, left London in 1850, and before its return to our more genial shores made one of the greatest discoveries of the century—that, namely, of the North-West Passage. The scene reproduced at the Exhibition shows the ship Investigator nipped in an ice-pack, and the sledge parties preparing to leave the ship, with a view to reach the mainland over the ice-floes. They eventually succeeded in doing this; and, by passing from ocean to ocean, proved for the first time in the written history of the world the existence of that North-West Passage of which mariners had so long dreamed in, vain. The model in question is ingeniously fitted with the electric light, by the aid of which the visitor gets some idea of the fitful flashes of the Aurora Borealis which illuminate the long Arctic night, and of the welcome dawn which the month of April brings round. The iceberg is, on the whole, an interesting appendix to the Franklin relics, and helps the visitor to realise the great Arctic tragedy associated with that explorer's honoured name.

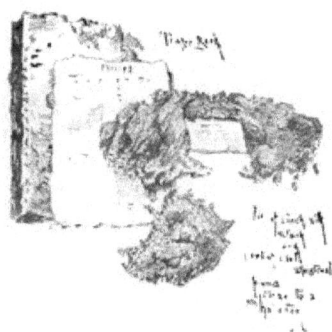

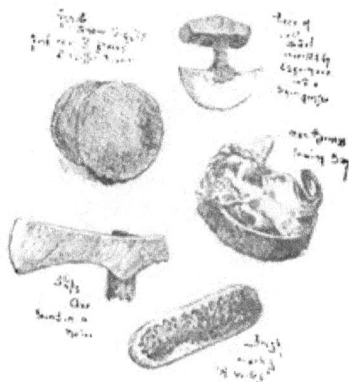

CHAPTER II.

BLAKE, NELSON, AND BENBOW GALLERIES.

THE PICTURE GALLERIES.

PASSING through the screen at the end of the Frank-lin Gallery, we find ourselves in the Nelson Gallery. Parallel to this, on the south (or left) side are the Blake and Benbow Galleries. In these three long rooms is contained the "Arts Section" of the Exhibition, which may be divided roughly into (1) Pictures, and (2) Relics. The Relics are in cases in the centre, and along the sides, of the Nelson and Blake Galleries, but it will be more convenient to treat the two classes of objects just specified in separate chapters.

We begin then with the collection of Naval Pictures, which is very rich alike in historical and artistic interest. As there are some 2,000 works to

Duke of Norfolk mentioned above (203) is one of the first we meet with, and is a good example of Holbein. A little further on is a fair example of one of the Van de Veldes (214). A large picture of the Spanish Armada, driven out of Calais Roads by Fire Ships (221), will attract attention. Near it is Mr. Sey-mour Lucas's picture of Don Pedro de Valdez delivering his sword to Sir Francis Drake (223), which many visitors will remember seeing in the Academy two years ago. Another striking Van de Velde represents the "Destruction of Dutch Ship-ping at Schelling, 1666" (281). This comes from the Queen's collection. The next picture (282), lent by Messrs. E. & E. Emanuel, of The Hard, Portsea,

223 THE SURRENDER: AN INCIDENT OF THE SPANISH ARMADA (SEYMOUR LUCAS).

be seen, any attempt to deal exhaustively with them here would be out of place. Those who wish to study them methodically must consult the Official Catalogue, where each of the pictures is described, and where, moreover, they are cast into progressive historical groups, thus assisting the studious visitor to turn the collection to full opportunity. On the walls of the three galleries are to be found portraits of nearly all the Naval Worthies of England, from Thomas Howard, third Duke of Norfolk, Lord High Admiral in the reign of Henry VIII., down to Lord Charles Beresford ; and representations of most of the Sea Fights from the days of the Spanish Armada to our own time.

The *numbers* on the pictures begin at the north-east end of the *Blake Gallery*, and continue round the walls (Nos. 201 to 449). The portrait of the

who are large contributors to the picture galleries, shows the Dutch Fleet conveying William of Orange to England. A picture by West, a former Pre-sident of the Royal Academy, which is sure to be noticed, shows the "Destruction of the French Ships in the Bay of La Hogue, after the Battle of Barfleur, 1692" (296). On the opposite wall there is a fine portrait by Reynolds of Admiral Keppel (342). "Rodney's Action with the French Fleet, 1782" (382) is a spirited picture : and so is De Leutherbourg's "Action of June 1, 1794" (464).

But the pictures which will attract most attention are those of Nelson's battles in the *Nelson Gallery*. In the centre of the left-hand wall is Mr. Baden-Powell's "Nelson at the Battle off St. Vincent" (311). The hero is represented boarding the Spanish man-

514. Commodore Nelson boarding the *San Nicolas* at the Battle off Cape St. Vincent, 1797. By Sir William Allan, R.A.

517. Commodore Nelson boarding the *San Josef* at the Battle off Cape St. Vincent, 1797. By G. Jones, R.A.

585. The Death of Nelson. By Daniel Maclise, R.A.

756. H.M.S. *Devastation*. By E. W. Cooke, R.A.

584. Battle off Cape Trafalgar, 1805. By J. M. W. Turner, R.A.

522. Nelson receiving the Swords of Spanish Officers on board the *San Josef*, at the Battle of Cape St. Vincent. By Barker.

708. Greenwich Pensioners at Nelson's Tomb in the Crypt of St. Paul's. By Sir J. E. Millais, R.A.

746. Commander Wyatt Rawson. By Caton Woodville.

511. Nelson at the Battle off Cape St. Vincent, 1797. By F. Baden-Powell.

739. Running the gauntlet on the Nile, between Matemneo and Khartoum. By S. Sufi.

of-war, at the moment of his famous exclamation "Victory or Westminster Abbey." A large picture of the same scene hangs close by (514); whilst Nos. 514 and 522 represent later incidents in the same engagement. In the centre of the opposite wall are three famous Trafalgar pictures, by Turner (584), West (585), and Maclise (586). The visitor will find it interesting to compare these pictures with the Panorama of the Battle which we shall see presently (Chapter XL).

Having made the circuit of the walls in the Nelson Gallery, the visitor should examine the screens, on which some of the best pictures in the Exhibition will be found. On the back of the third screen (counting from the end nearest to the main entrance) is a fine picture of "S.S. Teutonic, Armed Auxiliary Cruiser" (685).

Ruskin says that the great glory of the nineteenth century is that "it built ships of the line," and contrasts very unfavourably with the old wooden walls of England the men-of-war of to-day. But our latter-day artists have found beauty and grandeur in ironclads and gigantic "liners" no less than did their predecessors in the old broadsiders. On the whole, too, the visitor will probably be struck by the

THE ENGLISH FLEET ESCORTING PRINCE WILLIAM OF ORANGE TO ENGLAND. By P. Teglace.

superiority in sea-painting of the later artists. We must pass on, however, to call attention to Cooke's "Goodwin Sands" (705), (back of 5th screen); Millais' pathetic "Greenwich Pensioners at Nelson's Tomb" (708), (back of 6th screen); Wyllie's "Breaking up of H.M.S. Albion" (710), (front of 7th screen); Cooke's "Devastation" (755), (back of 8th screen); and the Egyptian War pictures (739), (back of 11th), and (746), (back of 12th). "Thumbnails" of some of the pictures we have mentioned will be found on the preceding page.

The visitor, having seen the Blake and Nelson Galleries, must now retrace his steps through the former into the Benbow Gallery, where there is a magnificent show of naval drawings, engravings, &c. Immediately on the left on entering this gallery is an interesting collection of drawings of Modern Battle Ships, lent by Lord Brassey. Some admirable water-colours by Brierly and others (1679 &c.) will next attract attention. But perhaps the most interesting "feature" of the Benbow Gallery is Mr. Grego's collection of caricatures &c. (on the screen at the far end), which illustrate in a very vivid way the rough social life of the Navy a century ago.

CHAPTER III.

BLAKE AND NELSON GALLERIES.

RELICS, &c.

RETURNING from the Benbow Gallery into "the Blake" and "the Nelson," we will next examine the relics and miscellaneous objects of art which are placed in these two Galleries. These objects are very numerous, and of very different degrees of interest. In the case of the relics, we fear we must add "and of doubtful authenticity." Let the visitor judge for himself. He will go over the *Victory* presently, and be able to form an idea of what the Admiral's cabin was like. It is simply a physical impossibility that it should have contained all the "favourite chairs," "arm-chairs," "chairs and beds combined," and "folding bedsteads" here exhibited as having been used by Nelson at sea. There is a similar difficulty with regard to "Nelson's" watches, seals, and medals. There are, however, enough well-authenticated relics of Nelson and other great commanders to make this part of the Exhibition very interesting. Unfortunately, however, it is for the most part arranged "anyhow." The Official Catalogue is full, but as the numbers in the cases are promiscuous, it is very difficult to find any par-

ticular object which one may be curious to see. All that we can attempt to do here is to give the reader a rough, general idea of the arrangement.

Beginning then in the BLAKE GALLERY at the end nearest the main entrance, and following the line of show-cases along the walls, we find along the wall on our left little of special interest. The cases here are devoted mainly to documents, medals, presentation swords and dirks. Along the opposite wall there are first more swords and then some interesting relics of Captain Cook—such as his cabinet (3150) and waistcoat (3180: see p. 16). Then in a further case are his rings, orders, seals, autographs, journal, &c. The next case is devoted to relics of Earl St. Vincent (his sword, spectacles, &c., see p. 14). The Collingwood relics are close by, including his telescope (3393: see p. 14). At the end of this wall are some gorgeous trappings belonging to the Cinque Ports; what a fine figure Warden W. H.

TROPHY OF 84 GUINEAS FOUND IN THE POSSESSION OF NELSON AT THE BATTLE OF TRAFALGAR.

Smith would cut in them! The Cinque Ports, it should be remembered, were originally responsible for the British navy. The principalships upon which the king had to rely until the fourteenth century were those which the five towns—Hastings, Sandwich, Dover, Romney, and Hythe—had by their charters to provide. We must pass on, however, to notice the cases in the middle of the gallery. These contain as follows:—No. 1, maces; No. 2, records;

Nelson's Teapot

GOLD DRINKING-CUP.

Sword presented to Lord Nelson by Spanish Admiral Don Xavier Winthuysen

Lord Nelson's Pistols

Lord Nelson's Pigtail cut off after death

The Bullet by which Nelson was killed

The Watch Lord Nelson wore at Trafalgar

Lord Nelson's Spy Glass

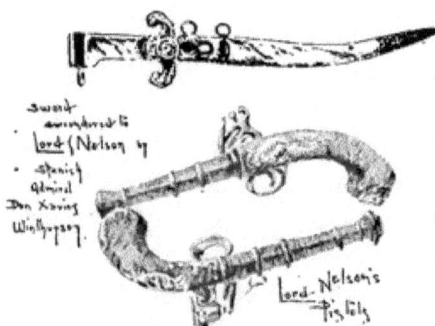

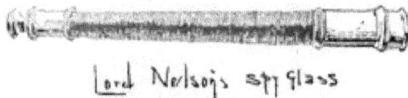

No. 3, miniatures ; No. 4, mugs ; No. 5, documents. Then comes (No. 6) a magnificent collection of silver-gilt models of ships lent by the Duke of Edinburgh. On either side of this case stand the silver models of the *Britannia* and the *Victoria*, the Jubilee presents from the Navy to the Queen. A portion of the mast of the *Victory* comes next (3320 : see p. 13). The next case (No. 7) is full of plate, including the trophy made of 84 guineas which were found in Nelson's purse at Trafalgar (3098 : see p. 11), and a silver model of the yacht *Speranza*, exhibited by Messrs. E. & E. Emanuel, of Portsea. No. 8, autographs and papers ; No. 9, glass ; No. 10, miniatures ; No. 11, swords ; and No. 12, presentation plate.

We pass now into the NELSON GALLERY. The cases along the wall on our left contain swords and snuff-boxes. At the far end of the room is a collection of British war medals and decorations (2478). The cases along the next long wall are mainly devoted to *Nelson Relics*. Sketches of many of these accompany the present chapter. It is interesting to turn from the portrait of Nelson and the pictures of his victories, which hang on the wall above, to these relics—the clothes he wore, the trinkets he valued, and all the other personal belongings, which were part of his familiar life. Turning, to complete our survey, to the cases in the middle of the Gallery, we enumerate their contents as before :— Nos. 1 and 2, naval uniforms ; Nos. 3 and 4, autographs (including several of Nelson's) ; No. 5, Gazettes ; No. 6, autographs ; No. 7, naval papers ; Nos. 8 and 9, autographs (with more of Nelson's) ; and finally a collection of flags. The autographs of Nelson scattered among the cases are numerous and interesting. Here, for instance (2299), is the first letter written by him after the loss of his arm. It is addressed to Sir John Jervis, afterwards Earl St. Vincent :—"I hope," he writes, "you will be able to give me a frigate to convey the remains of my carcass to England. . . . You will excuse my scrawl, considering it is my first attempt." In another letter (2331), seven years later, Nelson describes his wounds :—"When I run over the undermentioned wounds—eye in Corsica, belly off Cape St. Vincent, arm at Teneriffe, and head in Egypt, I ought to be thankful what I am." A letter

The washstand Lord Nelson used on board the Victory

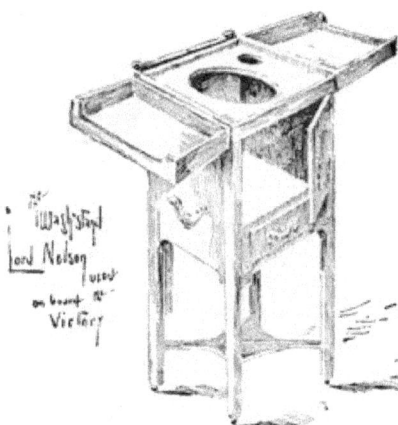

Used by Lord Nelson on board the Victory on the eve of Trafalgar

His one handed knife & fork

from Lieutenant John Pasco (2336), Signal Officer of the *Victory*, gives an account of Nelson's last telegraphic signal, and describes how the writer suggested the alteration of the word "confides" to "expects." A copy of the *Times* (2360) of Nov. 7, 1805, is interesting. It contains a list of the killed and wounded at the Battle of Trafalgar, and says :— "If ever there was a man who deserved to be praised, wept, and honoured by his country, it is Lord Nelson."

It is curious among so much that belonged to Nelson that there is no collection of relics of his "beloved Emma," the mistress of his heart who,

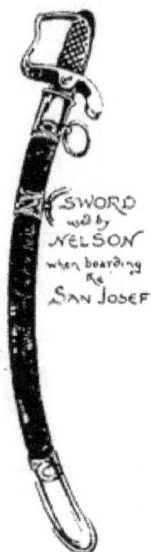

Sword used by NELSON when boarding the SAN JOSEF

NELSON'S COAT.

PORTION OF THE "VICTORY'S" MAINMAST, WITH SHOT-HOLE THROUGH.

in spite of all her failings, was one of the inspiring motives of his final heroism. "Was it, think you," asks Lowell, "of a tiny crooked outline on the map, of so many square miles of earth, that Nelson was thinking when he dictated what are perhaps the most inspiring words ever uttered by an Englishman to Englishmen? Surely it was something in woman's shape that rose before him with all the potent charm of noble impulsion that is hers as much through her weakness as her strength. And the features of that divine apparition, had they not been painted in every attitude of their changeful beauty by Romney?" One of these paintings will be found on page 40, together with a facsimile of the letter which Nelson wrote to her two days before his death.

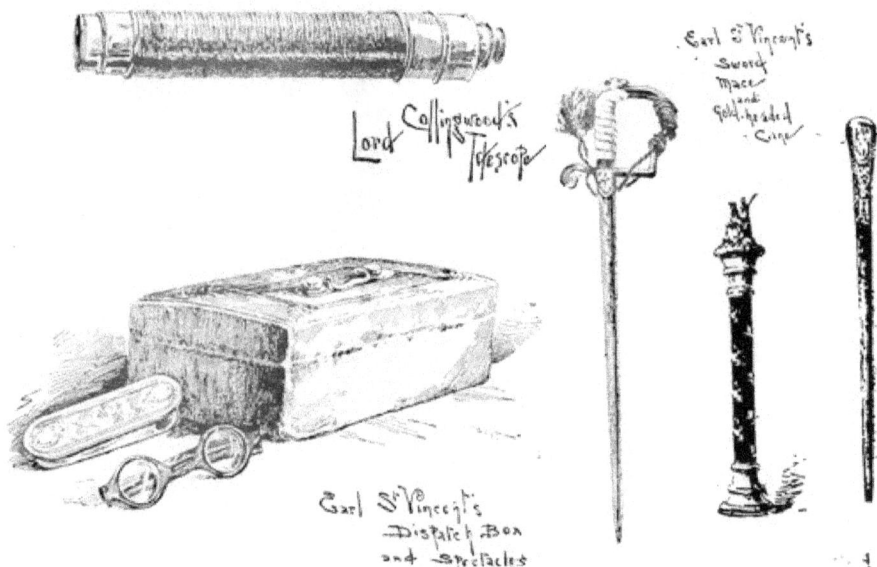

Lord Collingwood's Telescope

Earl St Vincent's Sword Mace and Gold-headed Cane

Earl St Vincent's Dispatch Box and Spectacles

LEAVING the Benbow, Blake, and Nelson Galleries, and therewith the Arts Section of the Exhibition, the visitor proceeds to the Howe Gallery, where the miscellaneous and "trade" exhibits are arranged. Most of these exhibits explain themselves, and are of the kind with which every Old Exhibition Hand will be familiar. The exhibits of most interest in strict connection with naval matters are those which deal with Victualling, but the victualling yards have not made the most of their opportunities. The old *Victory* has its sentimental interest, the new monster guns stir the imagination, and the pictures of sea fights rouse the latent Viking blood, but there is enough of the Saxon in us all to care for such a commonplace detail as Jack's rations. The skin-thatched sailor who stirs the pot in the Polar scene probably attracts as much attention as any of the other objects in the show, and had Deptford and the other yards been alive to their opportunities we should have had a cooking galley and Jack enjoying his salt junk and his ship biscuit. We have indeed some lay figures in uniform, but they do not suggest the agility and spryness of the A.B., and are, in short, "awful dead." Beyond these we have some grog tubs and mess kegs, which are not much to look at, with an uninteresting display of flour, pepper, cocoa, and other articles manufactured at the home victualling yards.

An old Jack Tar who had seen service in the Crimea was heard the other day to remark, after an inspection of the ship "stores" exhibited on a well-equipped stand in the Howe Gallery, that in his day they could make snuff-boxes of the "salt-junk" supplied to them, it was so old, hard, and black. Happily "Jack's" victuals have improved with the times.

It is in the training ship as a boy that the future Jack Tar first becomes acquainted with a scale of dietary that is so liberal as to be beyond the monetary reach of the class from which he is drawn. For John Bull wisely recognises that if he wants to turn out men of fine physique for his Navy, he must feed them when boys. That he does so let the following particulars show :—

Breakfast.—4 ozs. corned pork
8 ,, soft bread
½ ,, chocolate
½ ,, sugar

Dinner.—12 ozs. fresh mutton ⎫
12 ,, potatoes ⎬ Sunday
8 ,, flour ⎪ and
1 ,, fresh suet ⎭ Thursday
2 ,, raisins
12 ,, fresh beef ⎫ Monday
4 ,, bread ⎬ and
12 ,, potatoes ⎭ Friday
12 ,, fresh beef ⎫
12 ,, potatoes ⎬ Tuesday
4 ,, flour ⎪ and
½ ,, fresh suet ⎭ Saturday
8 ,, mixed vegetables

12 ozs. corned pork ⎫
4 ,, bread ⎬ Wednesday
12 ,, potatoes ⎪
4 ,, split peas ⎭
Tea.—10 ,, bread
½ ,, tea
1 ,, sugar

Supper.—4 ozs. bread (with dripping).

When the boy finally leaves the training ship and goes to sea his rations are somewhat different, but they are still on a liberal scale. Then he gets :—

Daily ⎰ Biscuit, 1½ lb.
⎱ or
Soft bread, 1½ lb.
Sugar, 2 ozs.
Chocolate, 1 oz.
Tea, ¼ oz.

Weekly ⎰ Oatmeal, 3 ozs.
⎱ Mustard, ½ oz.
Pepper, ¼ ,,
Vinegar, ½ pint

Daily ⎰ Fresh meat, 1 lb.
(when procurable) ⎱ Vegetables, ½ ,,

Every other ⎰ Salt pork, 1 lb.
day ⎱ Split peas, ½ ,,
Celery seed, ½ oz. to every 8 lbs. of split peas put into the coppers

On one ⎰ Salt beef, 1 lb.
alternate day. ⎱ Flour, 9 ozs.
Suet, ½ oz.
Raisins, 1½ oz.

On the other alternate day. ⎰ Preserved meat, ¾ lb. ⎱ with either
(1) Preserved potato, 4 ozs.
or
(2) Rice, 4 ozs.
or
(3) ⎰ Preserved potato, 2 ozs. ⎱ and
Rice, 2 ozs.
or
Flour, 9 ozs.
Suet, ½ oz.
Raisins, 1½ oz.

Although every inducement is held out to Jack, by the offer of additional rations of tea, sugar, &c., or their money value, to abstain from spirituous liquors, he gets, should he prefer not to be a teetotaler, a daily allowance of one-eighth of a pint of rum. This is his dietary when in health, and if he falls sick he is provided with delicacies in the shape of wine, calf's-foot jelly, fowl, beef-tea, and so on. With respect to quality all the stores are of the very best description, and every care is taken by the victualling yards to see that they are put on board ship in as perfect a condition as possible. The salt meat undergoes a rigid scrutiny before it is received into store by the officials, and if there is the slightest suspicion that it is not what it ought to be, it is immediately rejected. With respect to the officers, they are only entitled to draw the ration of the ordinary seaman, and in lieu thereof they obtain a money equivalent, which is put into the mess fund. Beyond providing some mess traps, the Admiralty leave the officers to cater for themselves.

CHAPTER V.

THE COOK GALLERY.—NAVIGATION.

If you want to know what modern science has done for the art of navigation, pay a visit to the Cook Gallery—in which you will find yourself if you pass through the Howe—and observe with care the many interesting exhibits which it contains. Roughly speaking, the Gallery consists of seven sections, one of which—the Arctic section—is referred to elsewhere (vide p. 5). Another is devoted to signals and the art of signalling at sea : a third to lights, buoys, and beacons ; a fourth to marine meteorology, a most important branch of practical science ; a fifth to hydrography or charts ; a sixth to compasses ; and a seventh to the instruments used in navigation.

CAPTAIN COOK'S WAISTCOAT.

First in importance among the exhibits comes Mr. Arthur Clayden's Ocean Current Models (4152). There are a pair of these ingenious contrivances perpetually on view in the Exhibition. The first shows in graphic fashion the course and character of the great ocean currents of the Atlantic ; the second deals with those of a more confined area—with those, namely, of the Indian Ocean. The former consists of a flat wooden tray, measuring about 21 inches by 30 inches, with a polished mahogany rim forming a sort of frame to the map which covers the bottom. This is a map (on Mercator's projection) of the Atlantic, the land masses being cut out of wood by a fret-saw, and fixed so that their flat surfaces stand about half an inch above the intervening parts of the tray. The smaller islands are represented by pins, wires, and bits of metal driven into the base board. On filling the parts which represent the ocean with water we have an ordinary map of the Atlantic with a surface of real water representing the sea. The wind (we quote here and there from Mr. Clayden's own description of the model) is a flat box fixed to the underside of the tray, and a number of tubes are brought up from it through the various continents and then bent over so that air issuing from them may blow over the model sea as the winds are known to blow in nature. Air is forced into the box by means of a foot blower, and it issues from all the tubes equally. In order to represent the difference between such strong and persistent winds as the Trades and the variable winds of our own latitudes, the Trade wind tubes are placed close together and their ends are brought near to the water so that the air-jet acts strongly. The tubes which bring our westerly winds, on the contrary, are directed so that the air-jets are considerably dispersed before they impinge upon the liquid surface. But the wind and the water are not in themselves sufficient to represent in a striking enough manner what really takes place. To indicate motion, Mr. Clayden has scattered lycopodium powder over the water. This floats upon the surface, and shows in the most unmistakable fashion the direction in which the currents flow.

CAPTAIN COOK'S SPEAKING TRUMPET.

MR. A. W. CLAYDEN'S WORKING MODEL, SHOWING THE CIRCULATION OF OCEAN CURRENTS.

Leaving this interesting model to the animated group of visitors which always surrounds it, we may with advantage glance for a moment at the models of the four Eddystone lighthouses (4106 et seq.). Here are faithful reproductions of Winstanley's lighthouse (1698), of Rudyard's lighthouse (1708), of Smeaton's lighthouse (1759), and of the present Eddystone lighthouse (1881). These are but a few of the many models grouped together in the section under notice. Not far from them is chronological collection of chronometers. Here may be found the timekeeper which gained for Harrison, its inventor, a reward of £20,000, and in this department also may be seen some of the best handiwork of Dent.

CHAPTER VI.

THE SEPPINGS.GALLERY: MODELS OF THE NAVY PAST AND PRESENT.

DESCENDING by the steps at the end of the Cook Gallery, the visitor finds himself in a long gallery

AN OLD SHIP'S GALLEY AND CREW.

AN OLD SLOOP OF WAR.

named after Sir Robert Seppings, an eminent naval architect in the reign of George IV., who introduced the principle of diagonal bracing. This is one of the most interesting galleries in the Exhibition, for it includes not only models of ships' engines, which will fascinate all visitors of a mechanical turn, but also the largest and most representative collection of models of the ships themselves ever brought together. Here, as in the Picture Galleries, to the visitor who wishes to "do" the Exhibition with remorseless thoroughness, the official catalogue is indispensable. Some 600 or 700 models are on view, and in that catalogue they will all be found enumerated.

The "general visitor," however, will probably content himself with a mere cursory inspection — walking through the gallery, and marking as he goes the historical developments

which have revolutionised alike our men-of-war and our merchantmen. The models, it should be observed, include two classes ; *first*, war ships, belonging mainly to the British navy ; *secondly*, ships

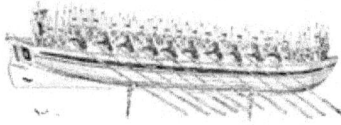

"THE GREAT HARRY." HENRY VIII.'s REIGN.

exhibited by the various shipbuilding firms and shipping lines in the British Empire. These latter models include several war-ships belonging to foreign navies. Thus Laird Brothers, of the Birkenhead Iron Works, exhibit (4315) several of the South American war vessels. In this second division of the models there is no attempt at historical completeness. The object of the various builders and owners is naturally to exhibit their latest and finest vessels.

The collection of models of ships in the British navy, though far from complete, and though not arranged very neatly, is nevertheless of great interest. The earliest of the vessels represented is the *Great Harry* (4695). The *Royal Sovereign* is a type of ships in the next century. Of 18th century ships there are several specimens ; and of the successive developments of naval architecture during the present century there is a complete illustration. From the spectacular

"THE VANGUARD." MODEL OF A SAILING LINE-OF-BATTLE SHIP OF 1835.

B

MODEL OF CAPTAIN COOK'S SHIP "RESOLUTION."

point of view, the models of the old "ships of the line" of 50 years ago—such as the *Vanguard*, of which we give an illustration—will attract the visitor's admiration. The scientific interest begins with the gradual alteration of the old model of a war-ship to steam propulsion and iron armament. The first sea-going iron armour-clad in the British Navy was the *Warrior*, built by the Thames Ship-building Company. The *Camperdown*, launched a quarter of a century later, is almost as different from the *Warrior* as the *Warrior* is from the *Vanguard*. But, indeed, the visitor will be reminded at every turn as he walks through this gallery of what was said by Sir Thomas Farrer the other day, that fashions are as changeable in war-ships as in ladies' bonnets.

In the large cases, in the middle of the gallery at its lower end, will be found a representation of the

MODEL OF THE WHITE STAR LINE ARMED CRUISERS, "TEUTONIC" AND "MAJESTIC."

MODEL OF THE ORIENT LINER S.S. "ORMUZ," 6,031 TONS, 8,500 HORSE-POWER.

Royal Navy in 1891—one case showing a Royal Review at Spithead ; another the various fleets grouped according to their respective stations throughout the world. The sketches and photographic reproductions which we give in this chapter illustrate some of the leading types of obsolete and present-day vessels, and may thus be interesting as a souvenir of this unique representation of the Navy Past and Present.   The Exhibition authorities remark by the way, that as " ships often undergo many changes in rig, armament, and appearance, during their existence, officers and men who have served in the ships must be prepared to find in the models occasional variations from the conditions with which they were familiar in the ships." The pictures of the *Camperdown, Volage,* and *Calypso, Boomerang, Katoomba* and *Latona,* are from photo-graphs kindly supplied by Messrs. Symonds & Co., of 39 High Street, Portsmouth, the well-known naval photographers. (It is to them also that we owe the photographic reproductions in the chapter on the *Victory.*) It should be added that another model—the most perfect perhaps in the Exhibition—will be found later on in the Armstrong Gallery. A visitor who wishes to realise to the full the difference between the old and new con-ditions cannot do better than carefully compare the old *Victory* with the new *Victoria* in the Armstrong Gallery (see p. 61.)

MODEL OF H.M.S. ''ACHILLES,'' IRONCLAD.

H.M.S. ''CAMPERDOWN,'' 10 GUNS, 10,600 TONS, 11,500 HORSE-POWER.   OF THE ''ADMIRAL CLASS.''
(THE FLAGSHIP OF THE CHANNEL SQUADRON.)

H.M.S. "VOLAGE," AND H.M.S. "CALYPSO" CHASING.   PART OF THE TRAINING SQUADRON, WEST INDIES.

H.M.S. "BOOMERANG," 1st CLASS TORPEDO GUN-BOAT, 735 TONS, 4,500 HORSE-POWER.

H.M.S. "LATONA," ONE OF THE SWIFTEST SHIPS IN THE ROYAL NAVY, 3,400 TONS, 9,000 HORSE-POWER.

H.M.S. "KATOOMBA," 2nd CLASS PROTECTED CRUISER, ONE OF THE NEW AUSTRALIAN SQUADRON, 2,575 TONS, 7,500 HORSE-POWER.

CHAPTER VII.

THE MODEL OF THE EDDYSTONE LIGHTHOUSE.

IN our tour of the Galleries we have now returned to the main entrance, and must make "a new departure" by passing into the grounds. Here we at once see, towering above us, the full-size model of the present Eddystone Lighthouse—the Eiffel Tower, as it were, of the Naval Exhibition. This belongs not to the executive of the Exhibition, but to Mr. David Charteris, a builder, of Earl Street, Westminster. The following is an account, in the shape of an interview with the builder, of this interesting model :—

"The framework consists of six rolled-iron ribs, each of which is placed in the angle of a hexagon, the whole being braced together by 'angle-irons' and flat bars. The height of the lighthouse—170 ft.—is divided into thirteen 'bays,' which correspond to the floors in the original structure. The foundations have been carefully laid, and the stability of the model is almost perfect. Each main rib is anchored by six large iron bolts to plates embedded in concrete twenty feet thick. Consequently the oscillation, even in a gale, is almost imperceptible.

"The whole of the model is covered with Portland cement coloured to resemble stone. Every joint in the original is carefully reproduced. The plaster which encases the model is spread upon expanded metal lathing—a recent invention particularly well adapted for holding the plaster. This lathing is made by cutting numerous slits in a sheet of iron, which is subsequently stretched. A piece of metal six inches wide may thus be expanded to the extent of three feet."

"At the top I see you have a lantern ; is this also a reproduction of the original?"—"In everything except the light. It is 14 ft. in diameter, and 16 ft. 6 in. high, and it is glazed with diamond panes just like the real lighthouse. The light, however, is a far more powerful one than that in use off the

THE EDDYSTONE LIGHTHOUSE.

Devonshire coast. At Eddystone they have lamps of about 25,000 candle-power ; we have one of the most brilliant arc lights ever made. At present its strength is that of about two million candles ; but soon we hope to raise it to five or even seven millions. The light revolves in periods of thirty seconds, the two flashes being separated by an interval of four seconds, and the groups by an interval of about twenty-one seconds. The electric lamps themselves are well worth looking at ; but, besides this, there is a balcony all round the lantern, from which a surprisingly beautiful view may be obtained. A strong wire netting is being placed around this balcony, so there need be no fear of accidents."

"They had a post-office at the top of the Eiffel Tower ; are you going to do anything in that line?"—"Certainly. We have arranged to sell special postcards at the top of the lighthouse, and visitors will have the satisfaction of posting their messages some hundred and seventy feet above the ground. The Post Office authorities have prepared a special stamp with which to obliterate the stamp upon the card.

"A specially-constructed hydraulic lift, which has been made by Waygood, is noteworthy for its safety and for economy in working. There are two cars, each capable of carrying eight persons at a time, one ascending as the other descends. Under each car is a tank, of a capacity to hold a sufficient weight of water to counterbalance the weight of the other car when loaded, and to overcome friction. The tank under the car which happens to be at the top is filled from a storage tank by means of a valve, under the control of the attendant, until the weight is sufficient to start the bottom car, when the valve closes itself automatically, and on reaching the bottom the water is automatically discharged into an exhaust tank, and pumped again to the storage tank at the top. Only sufficient water is used each journey to raise the excess of load in the ascending car, and if the descending load is the heavier no water at all is used. The lift is controlled by two of Waygood's Patent Long-stroke Jiggers, which enable the attendant to stop anywhere and as gradually as required."

"The lift is quite safe, I suppose?" — "Absolutely. The three wire cables by which the cars are connected are together equal to a strain of twenty-seven tons. Each 'cage' is also supported by four ropes, each rope being sufficiently strong to support the entire load. In the very remote event of the ropes breaking, powerful clutches

THE LIGHT AT THE TOP.

would at once grip the vertical 'guides,' and the car would not fall more than an inch before being brought to rest. You can't have anything safer."

"Now, Mr. Charteris, for a few figures to wind up with. How big is the model?"—"It is exactly the same size as that which now stands on Eddystone Rock—that is to say, the height from the ground to the top of the lantern roof is about 170 ft., while the base is 44 ft. in diameter and 19 ft. high.

Viewed from outside, it does not appear so high as it really is. This is because it is rather disadvantageously situated in the lowest part of Chelsea, the gardens being considerably lower than many of the streets in the neighbourhood. Nearly a hundred tons of iron and steel have been employed in its construction. There were more than a thousand pieces, every one of which was drilled, bent, and cut ready to be put in its place. All we had to do, therefore, was to piece the huge skeleton together and put flesh upon its bones. This, as everybody may see, has now been done." The Eddystone model is well worth ascending, we may add, apart from its intrinsic interest, for the sake of the magnificent bird's-eye view which, on a fine day, may be seen from the summit.

THE LIFT TO THE TOP.

AT THE TOP OF THE LIFT.

CHAPTER VIII.

A CHAT ON BOARD THE M.D.S.F.'S "HEROINE."

HE next object in a line with the Eddystone Lighthouse is the *Heroine*, a North Sea trawler, which the visitor may inspect at pleasure. It is glory — safe glory, in Charles Reade's phrase. If you have ever trawled in the North Sea, good fellow landlubber, you will appreciate the value of that. The *Heroine* is a trawler, all her canvas is up, and a fine head wind is blowing, but she is safely moored. So up you jump the steady steps at her side, and in another minute you lean against the bulwark in a talk with the jovial skipper of the smack which has caught fish for over thirty years, and which now is spending her remaining days in "catching men." There is something pathetic in the appearance of a worn-out boat, and though the *Heroine* in her old days is crowned with the glory of being one of the most attractive and popular exhibits at a great naval exhibition, there is still something about the air of the lumbering vessel that makes one feel rather sorry for her. The skipper *pro tem.* shares this sentiment. He said, looking over the bulwark :

THE YARMOUTH TRAWLER, "HEROINE."

"That's where she'll go—where she'll come to grief. Just on 'the line where she touches the ground. Below and above that she's all right, but she'll rot just there. "But she is not by any means an old vessel," he went on. "She has been at sea for thirty-three years only. That is not old as fishing smacks go. I have worked on one that had been to sea fifty-two years. It depends chiefly on what storms they have to weather. Why, only last year the *Heroine* was a first-class smack, but this last dreadful winter has done for her. She came home badly damaged, was put up for auction at Yarmouth, and the Mission to Deep-Sea Fishermen bought her on purpose for this Exhibition.'

"Now, what has the M.D.S.F. to do with smacks? Has it improved the trawling?"—"Not the trawling, but the trawlers." And here our skipper, who shares

the shortcoming (or is it a virtue?) of his tribe, or being without "the gift of the gab," warmed to his subject. "I have lived on a smack since I was a boy, and I know from experience of the change that has come over the fleets since the Mission came into existence, nearly ten years ago. Since then the grog and the gin are no longer the curses of the fleet ; since then the men live decent lives, and come home after eight weeks on the fishing ground, not half crazy with drink, and with empty pockets and brutal tempers, but soberly and steadily, and to homes which are no longer poverty-stricken, and wives and children no longer starved. There is no more madness, and despair, and suicide on board the smack, now that the devil of drink is there no more. And it is the Mission that has done it."

"How did it do it? Were the smacksmen more open to the teachings of tracts than the rest of this perverse generation?"—"No ; it was not the tracts alone that did it, though they too, and other books, have done and are doing their part of the work. Smacksmen, when there's no wind, have a good many free hours out at sea. Formerly they gambled and drank and smoked : now they read. The Mission vessels bring us books, and books are a boon greater than people imagine to those who live on the water. But they had more certain means than books to keep the fishermen from drink. You know who supplied the drink before the Mission came, don't you? It was the Dutch *coper*, a kind of floating tobacconist's shop. No smacksman can do without his 'baccy ;' the coper sold it to them, and when they came for their tobacco they were offered drink. Not even pure spirits it was what they sold, but adulterated nasty stuff that made you thirsty and crave for more and more till you lost your senses and became mad and brutal.

"The Mission people came ; they know that no smacksman would do without his pipe, and that he could buy his tobacco only from the coper. What did they do? They got permission from the Government to take out tobacco on the Mission vessels which were started, one after the other ; their tobacco was better and cheaper than that of the coper, and gradually they have drawn the gin shop of the coper out of the fleet."

Then a new large party of visitors climbed on board. The skipper went to meet them, to give information and booklets, and we climbed down what is a very primitive "companion" to where, below, another enthusiastic exponent to the advantages to the fishing fleets of the Mission is stationed to explain the mysteries of the bunks and the hold. A model of an invalided smacksman, strapped on a stretcher and carefully bandaged, supplies the theme to the eloquent guide through this department. He tells, as one who knows, of the awful sufferings the smacksmen had to under-

THE CABIN OF THE "HEROINE."

go in the past when an accident happened on board.

The Mission saw the pity of it all, and made it one of its main objects to train the skipper on every Mission smack in the elementary knowledge of nursing, bandaging, and ambulance work in general. Not long and every man in the twelve fleets trawling on the North Sea knew of the "doctor" on board the Mission smacks, and that, if a flag was hoisted and lowered three times on any smack, the Mission vessel would come alongside, and the patient would be attended to. Now the medical work has grown, and there are three hospital ships, with qualified medical practitioners on board, at work among the 20,000 men and youths on the North Sea.

MISSION TO DEEP-SEA FISHERMEN.
Patron, THE QUEEN.

IN HOSPITAL ON THE MISSION SMACK

CHAPTER IX.

THE SHOOTING GALLERY.

WE come next to what is a standing feature in these Exhibitions—the Shooting Gallery. If you have ever been inclined to doubt that Don Quixote was a truthful man when he declared that fighting windmills was exciting sport, go and look at the sportsmen —aye, and sportswomen too—at Messrs. Lyons' shooting gallery, and you will beg pardon of Sancho's master. To explain this suggestion we must tell something about the jungle and all that therein is. It—the jungle—is made of cardboard mainly, though you would not think so, looking at it. It begins just above the heads of the sportsmen who shoot ("Penny a shot, hit or miss") from behind a counter. You must not ask for such stupid details as, for instance, where the luxurious foliage over your head has grown up from ; let it suffice you that it is there. The fun begins with the fine jungle lake, which abounds in ducks—wild ones, we should say, judging by their size; there are foxes, too, and rabbits, and monkeys hanging in mid-air; and yet another creature, upon the nature of which we could never decide, till one morning, before Mr. Skinner, the contractor and superintendent of the jungle, got too busy to answer questions, we approached him as the best authority with the question—

"What is that nimble creature behind the second lake—a glorified guinea pig?"

"No," he answered with majestic calm, "it's a rat."

"And what are the animals made of?"

"Tin."

"And are the blue foxes and the glorified rats tinpots too?"

"Yes, all tin, painted over. It would never do to have anything less durable. As it is, they have all to be frequently replaced."

"What makes them move along so smoothly?"

"It is done by gravitation ; they are all on a line ; eight ducks, four foxes, and so on. The speed of each lot is regulated so as to suit all sportsmen."

"Has your sportsman a special fancy for any one creature?"

"Yes, he has, decidedly. First, as I told you, he shoots at the ducks because they travel slowly— offer better aim, you know. But he likes the rabbits too, and the monkeys are popular. The ladies were formerly always shooting at the owls. They like owls best. We had to do away with them—the owls, not the ladies — because there was some difficulty about fixing them up again when they were hit. All the animals hang on hinges and get up by themselves after they are hit."

"Not encouraging to the sportsman, is it? So you have ladies among your patrons, too. What kind of ladies?

"Why, bless you, we've lots of ladies : from the Princess of Wales and her daughters downwards. They came in and had a shot when they visited the Exhibition a week or two ago ; and of course the Prince and the Duke of Clarence tried their skill."

"It is amusing," continued Mr. Skinner, "to see people come in, trying their skill, who do not know how to handle a gun at all. But don't think we only get bad or indifferent shots here. Only yesterday a gentleman was here who hit a rabbit seventy-three times running."

THE SHOOTING GALLERY.

CHAPTER X.

THE "PENINSULAR AND ORIENTAL" PAVILION.

THE next "outside show" is one of the prettiest and most interesting in the Exhibition. This is the P. and O. Pavilion, of which, however, it is un-

"WILLIAM FAWCETT," S.S., THE FIRST OF THE P. AND O. STEAM LINERS.

necessary to say anything here, for on entering you will find courteous attendants to "tell you all about it," and a special book may be had describing the history and operations of this great company. We are, however, able, by the kindness of the artist, Mr. Frank Murray, to give illustrations showing the frieze which runs round the dome. The frieze is in eight panels, each panel about twelve feet long by three feet high. Four panels, at the opposite points of the compass, represent the four quarters of the globe. The four inter-mediate and alternating panels form a series deal-ing with four represen-tative epochs of shipping. Commencing with com-pass-point panels, the western, facing the main entrance, shows a vessel of the P. and O. fleet off Gibraltar; the northern, Arctic scenery, with an early 17th century ship surrounded by icebergs; the southern, a modern three-masted whaling

clipper, with all sail set, in southern seas; the eastern, Malay, Japanese, and Chinese junks and prahns. The historical series begins with a fleet of Viking ships of the 10th century setting forth from port on an expedition. The principal boat is well under weigh; the others are hoisting sail. The next panel —end of the 15th century — represents the caravels of Colum-bus at the dawn of the 12th of October, 1492, the *Santa Maria*, the *Pinta*, and the *Nina*. Though some liberties had to be taken for the sake of decorative effect, the vessels may be taken to be fairly representative of the celebrated caravels of that place and time. The next subject is a group of Mediterranean galleys of the 17th century.

THE P. AND O. PAVILION. *Designed by Mr. Colcutt.*

The background is taken from the port of Rhodes. These oared vessels form a special class of extreme interest. Every detail of their make, fitting, rigging, and manœuvre is obtainable. The last subject is a three-decker of the largest size, mounting 100 guns,

body, the light reflected from the metal surface passes through them in precisely the same way that light

TENTH-CENTURY VIKING SHIPS.

date about 1760, representative of the highest type of vessel of war before the age of steam. The paintings

passes through a stained-glass window. The small number of good glazing colours, and the slight opacity

CARAVELS OF COLUMBUS.   FIFTEENTH CENTURY.

are in oil-colour on canvas, stretched on frames, and painted on gold and silver grounds. The use of gold

that even the best have, impose certain limitations on their use ; but quite within their scope is sufficie

GALLEYS OF MEDITERRANEAN OFF RHODES.   SIXTEENTH CENTURY.

and silver as a ground gives an effect of luminous richness which ordinary solid oil painting cannot

variety of tone and shade for effective decorative use. A great part of the work in the frieze is painted

THREE-DECKER FRIGATE.   EIGHTEENTH CENTURY.

possibly reach. The colours used are almost entirely the kind known as "glaze." Having no solid opaque

as well in solid colour—the combination of solid and transparent painting gives a greater decorative range than either would alone. It may add to the interest attaching to these subjects to know that as far as others of which it must always be more or less a matter of conjecture as to their outer shapes,

NORTH POLE.

possible historical accuracy has been sought for in their details. The warships of the eighteenth century, though their working and outfit are fairly well known. Curiously enough, the war vessel of a much

SOUTHERN SEAS.

of course, present no difficulties in this way—nor the galleys of the late sixteenth and early seventeenth, earlier period can be realised easily. The Viking or Norse vessels of the tenth and eleventh centuries

EAST. MALAY PIRATES AND JUNKS.

When we come to the end of the fifteenth and the fourteenth centuries, one has to rely almost entirely can be reconstructed with great exactness—as two are in existence ; the Sagas give careful and exact

WEST. P. AND O., OFF GIBRALTAR.

on paintings and manuscripts. Certain types of vessel are to be found fairly well illustrated, and descriptions of them. These pictures of early ships usefully supplement those in the Exhibition Galleries.

CHAPTER XI.

THE PANORAMA OF THE BATTLE OF TRAFALGAR.

"1805, *Oct.* 21*st.* . . . *About* 1.15 *Lord Nelson was wounded in the shoulder.*" So runs the brief but significant record contained in the log of the *Victory.* The wound which caused the death of one of England's greatest admirals was officially chronicled in less than a dozen words. For fuller and more affecting accounts we must turn elsewhere. From these we learn that Captain Hardy and Lord Nelson were walking together on the quarter-deck, when suddenly the Admiral tottered and fell with his face on the boards. A musket-ball from the mizen-top of the *Redoutable* had passed downwards through his left epaulette and lodged in the spine ; the chaplain ran to him, but a sergeant and two sailors had already reached him and lifted him off the deck covered with the blood that stained it. Hardy, who had not heard the noise of his fall, turned round, and, pale and more stricken than Nelson himself, exclaimed, " I hope you are not dangerously wounded, my lord ?" " They have done for me at last, Hardy ; my back-bone is shot through."

The precise moment at which this happened is the moment chosen by the Chevalier Philipp Fleischer, in his panoramic representation of the battle of Trafalgar and death of Lord Nelson, now on view at the Royal Naval Exhibition. The painter shows the fight as its fortunes stood at a quarter past one on the twenty-first of October, 1805. He has consulted the most important works, historical and tactical, which have been written on the subject, and he has studied the logs of the various British ships which took part in the engagement. Models, uniforms, arms, and other contents of the naval museums have also been laid under contribution. It is claimed for the artist, who, by the way, is a

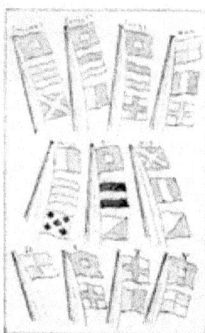

ENGLAND EXPECTS EVERY MAN
WILL DO HIS DUTY.

German hailing from Munich, that " in no single detail has he yielded to the temptation of sacrificing historical truth to pictorial effect." From the point of view of history, there is under these circumstances nothing left to be desired.

The Trafalgar Panorama, like the model of the Eddystone Lighthouse, is a private speculation. It is the property of Herr Thiem, who has already shown it at an exhibition in Edinburgh. It is exhibited in a polygonal building— a building which after the mimic lighthouse and the model of the *Victory*, forms one of the chief attractions of the Exhibition as seen from the outside. It is equally prominent when viewed from the grounds. No visitor can fail to see the many-angled structure ; and no visitor who desires to realise what a sea-fight was like in the days which preceded ironclads will, we venture to think, grudge the sixpence asked for a view of the picture contained within its walls. You pay your sixpence, and ascend a staircase, landing upon the aft part of the quarter-deck—the topmost of the five decks which spanned the length and breadth of the *Victory.* You look straight ahead towards the bow, and there, in the middle of the quarter-deck, you observe the great scene on account of which the picture was painted. You look upon Lord Nelson at the moment that he has fallen mortally wounded ; you see him raised by a seaman ; you notice Captain Hardy, sword in hand, turning with tender solicitude towards his chief ; and you see the sailor hurrying along with a sheet of canvas on which to carry the Admiral down to the cockpit.

PLAN OF THE BATTLE OF TRAFALGAR, SHEWING
THE POSITION OF THE FLEETS.
English Fleet ☐   French and Spanish Fleets ■

Note, in passing, that Lord Nelson is dressed in his old and somewhat threadbare frock uniform coat with four stars of different orders stitched on the left breast, his armless right sleeve being fastened to a front button. Had the French seaman, or marine, whose shot proved so fatal, been anxious to kill the British Commander-in-Chief, he would probably have aimed at Captain Hardy, who was far away the better dressed officer of the two. Most likely the musket was pointed at random. A moment's glance at the mizen-top of the *Redoutable* will reveal the

"BUCENTAURE," THE FRENCH ADMIRAL'S SHIP.
Her mainmast is falling, owing to the accurate firing of the *Conqueror*.

Frenchman who fired the shot. He and his companion did not long remain there. One of them was soon afterwards killed in the mizen-top; the other endeavouring to effect his escape from the top down

interest may be allowed to concentrate itself for a brief moment upon the striking scene which surrounds us.

Close at hand is the deck of the *Victory*, where,

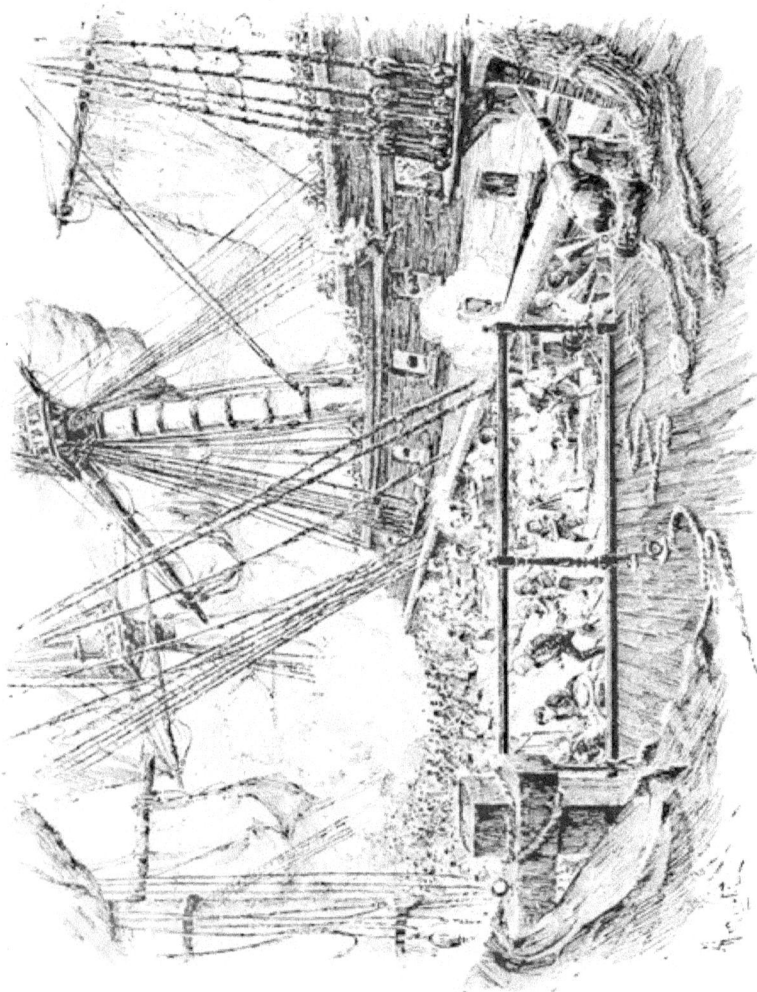

1.35 P.M.—ON BOARD THE "VICTORY."

the rigging, was shot by a midshipman, and fell dead from the shrouds.

By this time we may assume that Lord Nelson has been carried below to the cockpit—the death bed scene is described in the preceding article, and our

upon the right, or starboard side, the English gunners pour their volleys into the portholes of the *Redoubtable*. On the left side the port guns play upon a formidable Spanish four-decker. Captain Adair, of the Marines, may be seen in the foreground wisely commanding his men to disperse about the ship, so that they may not suffer so severely from the enemy's musketry. The *Redoutable* is terribly close at hand, and just beyond it is our own ship, the *Téméraire.* Upon the starboard side of the

But to enumerate all the ships—English, French and Spanish—which took part in this great naval engagement would require far more space than is just now at our disposal. The sea, which surrounds the spectator, is almost covered with ships of war

FOUR SHIPS OF THE LINE LOCKED TOGETHER. THE "VICTORY," "REDOUTABLE," "TÉMÉRAIRE," AND "FOUGUEUX."

Téméraire is another French ship, the *Fougueux*—which is expiating in the saddest fashion possible the ill-directed valour which sent her to assist her companion in distress.

For the spectator stands upon the deck of the *Victory*, and sees the ships as Nelson saw them ere he fell. The diagram on page 30 will give the reader an idea of the number and arrangement of the ships which took part in the historic fight. What the various ships looked like at the supreme moment when Nelson received the musket-ball may be seen by glancing at the panorama. To this reproduction of the battle upon canvas—canvas measuring 310 ft.

by 30½ ft.—we refer every reader who visits the Naval Exhibition. From this canvas reproduction and from the model of the *Victory* the visitor will learn in half an hour more than the ordinary history books can teach him in a year.

THE "ROYAL SOVEREIGN," WITH THE FLAG AT THE FOREMAST, IS VICE-ADMIRAL COLLINGWOOD'S SHIP.
After engaging four of the enemies' ships, the *Tonnant* comes to her assistance. On the right is the *Santa Anna*, the remains of the *Royal Sovereign's* first opponent.

CHAPTER XII.

THE MODEL OF H.M.S. "VICTORY."

LORD NELSON's flagship, the *Victory*, is at least a hundred and twenty-six years old. She is some 226 ft. in length from figure-head to taffrail, and in her widest part measures more than 50 ft. From water-line to bulwarks there is a distance of 40 feet. The model at Chelsea is not fully rigged, the County Council, for reasons best known to themselves, having objected to any reproduction of the three masts and the sails which carried the *Victory* into action on the fateful 21st of October, 1805. The flags fly, however, just as they did on the day when Nelson made the ever-memorable signal "England expects that every man will do his duty." With the exception of masts and rigging—things of no small importance—the Exhibition model is a perfect reproduction of the old ship. The many-windowed stern is a striking sight — especially from the Embankment—and so also is the figure-head. The latter consists of a marine on the port and a sailor on the starboard side, supporting a shield carrying the Royal Arms. The water-line, it may be noted, is clearly marked. The displacement of the *Victory* was considerably over two thousand tons.

Visitors to the Naval Exhibition are allowed to inspect the model free of charge. They enter by the entry port—as in the original—and pass in on to the middle or main deck. The *Victory*, like most of the ships of war built towards the close of

the eighteenth century, had five decks. At the very top was the quarter-deck, upon which Lord Nelson received his fatal wound, and beneath this was the upper deck. Neither of these is reproduced in the model. Next came the middle deck to which we are referring. Visitors pass from this deck down the gangway to the lower or fighting deck, which is shown in the Chelsea model just as it is supposed to have been on the morning of the battle of Trafalgar. On the port side the guns are run out ready for action; the cannon-balls, muskets, and other deadly apparatus of war being in their places. On the starboard side—that is to say, on the left of the spectator—are to be seen the mess-tables, forms, and hammocks which the sailors used when not actively engaged in fight. From this deck visitors descend to the lowest deck of all -the orlop deck—in which is situate the cockpit where Lord Nelson died. The accompanying sectional diagram will give some idea of the arrangement of decks usual when the *Victory* was built.

It is not easy for a tall person to walk in comfort along any of these decks, except the topmost one. All are low; all are badly lighted by horn lanterns, and nearly all are insufferably stuffy. The orlop deck, to which the wounded (including Nelson) were carried, lies, as

THE FIGURE-HEAD OF THE "VICTORY." STARBOARD.

THE FIGURE-HEAD OF THE "VICTORY." PORT.

LORD NELSON IN THE CABIN OF THE "VICTORY."

may be seen in the diagram, below the water-line. It was in the main a safe place, since the only danger incurred was one which would affect the ship as a whole, such as fire or foundering. The sufferings of the wounded as they lay at the bottom of the ship, maddened by the stifling heat and the noise of battle, and agonized by wounds which the skill of an overworked surgeon could but perfunctorily attend to, may be left to the imagination.

But what (it will be asked) were the armaments of the *Victory?*—what guns did she carry, and how were they worked? The total number of guns was 104. On the lower deck—the deck which, as we have before pointed out, saw most of the fighting— were thirty long 32-pounders. Upon the middle deck were thirty long 24-pounders; upon the main deck thirty-two long 12-pounders; upon the upper deck eight short 12-pounders and two 32-pounder carronades; and upon the forecastle two 68-pounder carronades. Each man worked at two guns, devoting his attention to corresponding guns on opposite sides of the ship. It does not require a very vivid imagination to conjure up a picture of the scene on board the lower deck of the *Victory* at the time of the great battle of Trafalgar. One can easily imagine the gunners rushing hither and thither, the shot tearing across the decks, killing and wounding as it speeds along its deadly course, the deafening crash of broadsides, and the universal stifling smoke. This was naval warfare in the days of Lord Nelson.

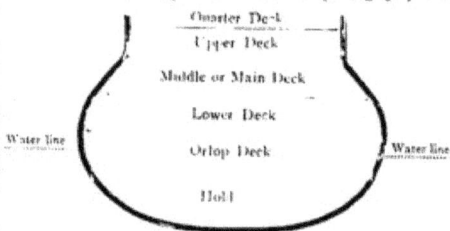

Let us turn for a moment to the comparative quiet of the orlop deck. To this haven there has been borne, along with the innumerable other sailors who have taken part in the glorious fight, the Admiral himself. Tenderly they carried him down the companion ladder, and softly they laid him in the cockpit. Here he lies mortally wounded— surrounded by his faithful chaplain, by the doctor whose skill can do no more for him, and by Captain Hardy. The deathbed scene has been faithfully reproduced in wax by Mr. John Tussaud, of the firm of Mdme. Tussaud & Sons.

The cockpit, in which the great sea-king lies dying, is dimly lighted by a horn lantern, while a sailor standing by holds another lantern, the light of which falls upon the hero's face. Nelson has been stripped of his clothes, and lies partially covered with a sheet. The moment may be assumed to be that at which

Quarter Deck
Upper Deck
Middle or Main Deck
Lower Deck
Water line
Orlop Deck
Water line
Hold

H.M.S. "VICTORY," NELSON'S FLAGSHIP.

NELSON WOUNDED AT THE BATTLE OF TRAFALGAR

Captain Hardy paid his second and last visit to his dying chief—the moment at which (as Dr. Beatty tells us) the Captain knelt down and kissed his cheek, while Nelson said: 'Now I am satisfied; thank God, I have done my duty.'" Hardy left; returning once more to the quarter-deck, where his presence was, of course, urgently needed, and Nelson remained with the chaplain and physician at his side. The end soon came. The musket-ball which flew from the mizen-top of the *Redoubtable* was winged with death. Hardy had not been long upon the quarter-deck, when Nelson murmured the words "God and my country," and passed quietly away.

THE LOWER DECK : MEN'S QUARTERS.

Mr. Tussaud in the course of a recent conversation. "It is to a very considerable extent founded upon a picture by Devis, now in Buckingham Palace. It is not, of course, a complete realisation of that picture in wax; but the 'reading' of the group—if I may so put it —is taken from it.

"I also studied every contemporary print and engraving upon which I could lay hands; I went down to the museum at Greenwich Hospital and inspected the Nelson relics; I examined the bust of Captain Hardy contained in Greenwich Church; I absorbed everything that was of value in Benjamin West's picture; and finally I consulted numerous old military and naval tailors and accoutrement

THE ORLOP DECK : OFFICERS' QUARTERS.

"How did you succeed in reproducing the last scene so faithfully?" inquired our representative of

makers, with a view to ensuring the most absolute correctness of costume."

"Well, having got all your materials, how did you set to work?"—"Here," replied Mr. Tussaud, "is my first study." The artist produced a representation of the group in modelling-wax done to a one-inch scale. "This," he continued, "is prepared with the object of seeing what the general effect of the group will be. If it satisfies us, as this did, all the figures are modelled, life-size, in clay. We work just like the ordinary sculptor, you see —employing life models and all the rest of it, as does the artist in marble."

"Assuming that the clay figures satisfy you, what happens next?"—"They are moulded, and those parts which are covered with clothes are cast in plaster. Wax would not stand the weight of costume or the strain which a tightly-buttoned coat or vest would impose upon it. Such parts of the figure as are intended to represent the flesh are reproduced in wax. These parts are generally the whole of the head and hands—in the case of the dying Nelson they include the bare breast. The figure being complete, the hair is inserted —a delicate operation, which if not properly performed is calculated seriously to affect the likeness."

THE MIDDLE DECK : CLEARED FOR ACTION.

DEATH OF NELSON. COCKPIT OF " VICTORY." *From the Picture by Davis.*

EMMA, LADY HAMILTON. *A portrait by Romney.*

ON the morning of the 19th of October, 1805, the combined fleets of France and Spain, lying in Cadiz harbour, began to get under way. At half-past nine A.M. a signal was made that the enemy's fleet was coming out of port. At three P.M. Nelson received the long-wished-for intelligence that they were at sea.] It was then that, rejoicing at the near approach of that moment he had so ardently awaited, Nelson penned the interesting document of which this is a facsimile. It was found open on his desk, together with one addressed to his daughter, Miss Horatio Nelson Thompson, now in the possession of Mrs. H. N. Ward. To the last writing of Nelson Lady Hamilton has added, "This Letter was found open on *his* desk, and brought to Lady Hamilton by Captain Hardy. Oh, miserable wretched Emma,— Oh, glorious and happy Nelson." The envelope containing these letters is superscribed "The enclosed letters were found after the action, and sealed up in the presence of the Rev. Mr. Scott, signed T. M. Hardy."

Victory Octr. 19th 1805
Noon Cadiz ESE 16 Leagues

My Dearest beloved Emma the dear friend of my bosom the Signal has been made that the Enemys combined fleet are coming out of Port. We have very little Wind so that I have no hopes of seeing them before tomorrow. May the God of Battles crown my Endeavours with success at all events I will take care that my name shall ever be most dear to you and Horatia both of whom I love as much as my own life, and as my last writing before the battle will be to you so I hope in God that I shall live to finish my letter after the

NELSON'S LAST LETTER.

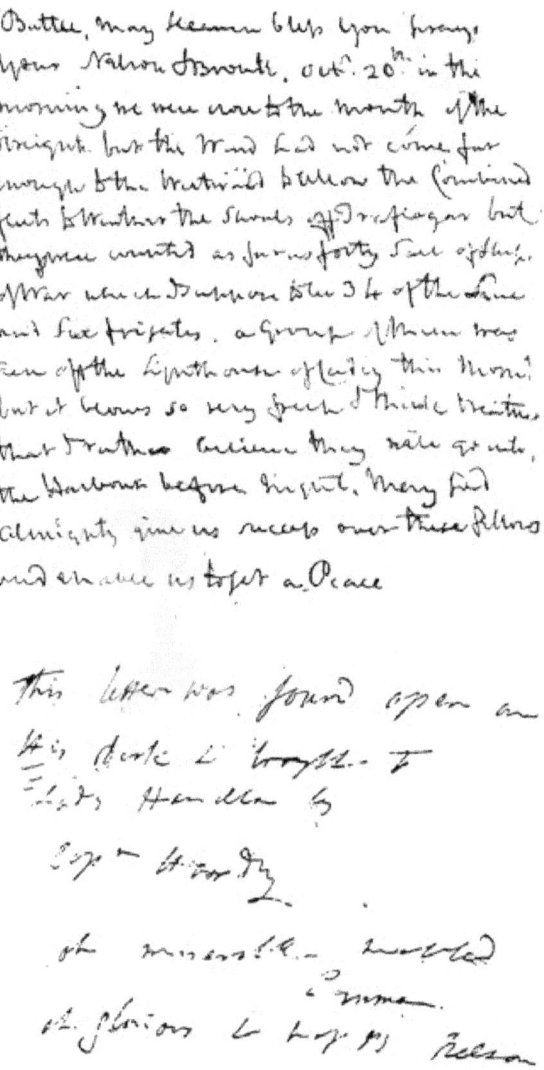

CHAPTER XIII.

THE CAMPERDOWN GALLERY.

DIVING AND TORPEDOES.

AFTER leaving the model of the *Victory*, we pass by the kiosk of the Thames Shipbuilding Company; and re-entering the Exhibition Galleries find ourselves in the Camperdown. The most interesting thing here is the diving tank. Every day it is surrounded by a crowd of spectators watching intently the evolutions of the man-monster in the diving-dress, who gambols about with as much ease and pleasure as a young and lively fish. He picks up coins, he writes on a slate, and he talks to you through the telephone. This dress combines all the latest improvements in the diver's equipment. Close to the tank is a case of relics from the deep. In the centre is an oak bowl made from the timbers of the *Royal George*, which (every one knows) went down off Spithead in 1782, and was brought up in bits by Mr. Siebe's men in 1844 (a fact of which few are aware). In the bowl are the sole of an old shoe, the ring from a dead man's finger, a black silk handkerchief, and other curiosities, which were brought up from the wreckage after lying at the bottom of the sea for sixty-two years. A fragile cup and saucer, recovered from an ancient East Indiaman which went down off the Cape of Good Hope in the seventeenth century; Greek wine jars encrusted with shells, dating centuries B.C.; a worm-eaten discoloured silver dish, also from the *Royal George*; a relic from the *Mary Rose*, sunk in 1545; a carpenter's plane, once used in the Spanish Armada, found in Vigo Bay—all these, and many more relics from the deep which have been found by divers, may be seen in that same glass case. The tank and the case, with other diving exhibits, are shown by the well-known firm of Siebe & Gorman, of Westminster Bridge Road. Mr. Siebe was called the father of the diving dress. Mr. Gorman is the present head of the firm, and he was good enough to give one of our representatives many of the facts in the following article:

THE SIEBE-GORMAN DIVING DRESS.

The Siebe-Gorman diving dress, as we see it to-day in the tank at the Naval Exhibition, is the development of the Siebe costume invented in 1837. The dress is used in all parts of the world, and all submarine operations. The diver must, therefore, be a practical man, able to turn his hand to any trade. Pier construction, wreck raising, submarine mining, the cleaning and repairing of ships, work in collieries and tunnels—in all such operations the diver is required.

THE DIVING TANK.

HOW DEEP IN THE DEEP.

Mr. Gorman has drawn up from his large experience a valuable paper on the art of diving. Here, for instance, is a table which shows the pressure on the square inch at a given depth of water:

10 fee.	....	4½ lbs.
20 "	....	8½ "
40 "	....	17½ "
30 "	....	21½ "
60 "	....	26½ "
70 "	....	30½ "
80 "	....	34½ "
90 "	....	39 "
100 "	....	43½ "
110 "	....	47½ "
120 "	....	52½ "
130 "	....	56½ "
140 "	....	60½ "
150 "	....	65½ "
	Limit	
160 "	....	69½ "
170 "	....	74 "
180 "	....	78 "
190 "	....	82½ "
*204 "	....	88½ "

* The greatest depth any diver has ever descended.

It is obvious that the least flaw in the construction of the dress would be fatal to the diver, and Mr. Gorman is very proud of the fact that no diver has died owing to faulty manufacture. The air pipes are tested to bear a pressure of 100 pounds to the square inch.

Here are a few examples of the romance of deep-sea diving—In August, 1869, the *Hamilla Mitchell* was lost on the Leuconna rock, near Shanghai, having a heavy cargo, and specie to the amount of £50,000. Lloyd's agent was instructed by the underwriters to visit the scene of the wreck, and inform them as to the feasibility of recovering the treasure. His report was that he considered the cargo and

A VARIETY OF WORK ACCOMPLISHED BY THE DIVER.

THE WRECK OF THE "ROYAL GEORGE."

The *Royal George*, 104 guns, sunk at Spithead in 1782, was recovered in 1844 under the direction of Major-General Pasley. This drawing represents divers at work on the wreck, who exclusively used the [improved] diving apparatus manufactured by Mr. A. Siebe, inventor of the close diving dress.

treasure irrevocably lost, as the depth of the water was so great and the position too dangerous for working. Captain Lodge, however, undertook the task, and having consulted the eminent submarine engineers, Messrs. Siebe & Gorman, as to the diving-gear he should require, they supplied him with one of their new diving apparatuses on a new principle, and specially constructed for deep-sea diving, and having engaged two experienced divers, Messrs. R. Ridyard and W. Penk, of Liverpool, Captain Lodge left England and arrived at Shanghai in the month of May last, where he engaged the pilot cutter *Maggie*, and proceeded in search of the wreck. This operation had to be prosecuted by means of a boat, as the larger vessel could not proceed so close to the high rocks. After a search in different depths, varying from 120 feet to 145 feet, the divers at length found the wreck. The after part, containing the treasure, had rolled into deep water, by 23 fathoms or thereabouts, for it appears that when the *Hamilla Mitchell* struck the rock she rested on a ledge, but subsequent gales caused her to part amidships, the after part rolling into deep water.

After some difficulty Ridyard succeeded in obtaining access to the treasure-room, when he found that some of the dollars were lying in heaps, the worms having eaten the wooden boxes so that they were completely riddled. Ridyard

RELICS FROM THE DEEP.
The Bowl is made from the *Royal George*.

made four successful trips, the last of which proved the most advantageous of all. During this time he worked four hours consecutively under water, and sent up the contents of sixty-four boxes of treasure. He returned exhausted to the boat from having worked so long at the great depth mentioned, a feat which was never performed by a diver before this occasion. Ridyard partially attributed his extraordinary success more particularly to the superiority of Messrs. Siebe & Gorman's apparatus than to his own personal exertions. Being thirsty, W. Penk volunteered to ascend to the top of the island to fetch him some spring water; but while filling the bucket he looked around the horizon, and to his astonishment he saw an innumerable quantity of white sails coming from the mainland. He informed Captain Lodge of the circumstance, and he identified them as several hundred piratical junks bearing down upon the island. Orders were therefore given to slip the anchor and chain, but the wind being light they were obliged to make use of oars; and, although in an exhausted condition, Ridyard pulled some time until a breeze sprang up, when they were enabled to make sail, and with the aid of night they reached Shanghai safely, running a very close risk not only of losing the treasure they had on board, but also their lives. The Shanghai papers blame the authorities for not giving them sufficient protection. The total amount of treasure recovered was £40,000, and if it had not been for this *contretemps* Ridyard had intended to have completed the entire salvage of the treasure that same day. Captain Lodge and his divers returned from their hazardous expedition in August last, having been six months from the time of leaving England until their return. The remaining amount of treasure was afterwards entirely recovered.

The ship *Cape Horn* was wrecked on the coast of South America with a cargo of copper, valued at £50,000, and an expedition was sent to attempt its recovery. The steamship *Santiago* was fitted up, and a diver named lame Hooper was engaged.

Upon their arrival at the scene of the wreck the sunken vessel was dragged for and found. Upon sounding, a depth of 34 fathoms was discovered around the wreck. Hooper, nothing daunted, declared his intention to descend, which he did seven times, and one time remained 43 minutes at a depth of 33 fathoms, or 201 ft. This is said to be the greatest depth ever attained.

SPONGE AND PEARL FISHERIES.

Within these last ten to fifteen years a large commerce has sprung up in the above fisheries, and this can only be attributed to the use of the diving apparatus, which is now daily becoming of greater importance for those purposes : formerly naked divers only were employed, and the result was only the recovery of a limited quantity, as the diver could not remain but a few seconds to collect, and then only in reach of his arms' length ; now the divers remain from two to four hours under water, collecting in that time what would have required twenty naked divers. In the sponge fishery in the Mediterranean waters there are employed over three hundred sets of diving apparatus, without reckoning the fisheries at the Bahamas, Bermuda, and off the coast of Australia and other parts of the world. The pearl fisheries are rapidly becoming of the greatest importance, not only for the pearls,

GREEK LAMP.
(Recovered from a depth of 140 feet. Sponge growing on top.)

but also for the shells, the last-named of a certain species fetching from £7 to £8 the cwt. The pearl oyster (classified as the *Avicula margaritifera*) is an oyster slightly larger than the European congener, and is valuable for the pearl it bears, the shells themselves being of no commercial value ; these are found more or less in all parts of the world, but more principally on the coasts of Ceylon, West Australia, Fiji Islands, Malacca Straits, and some parts of the coasts of the West India Islands. The pearl oyster (*Meleagrina margaritifera*) is valuable for the shells, only a pair of them weighing about two pounds. These are found in great quantities all over the north coast of Australia, and in the Malacca Straits and coasts of

Guinea large fisheries are now being conducted with considerable success and profit ; and, as the diving apparatus is now being more and more introduced into these fisheries, we may expect them to become a very important industry.

CORAL AND AMBER.

Coral has received as yet very little advancement from the use of the diving apparatus, and the fishermen seem at present bound to their ancient style of fishing. Whether it is the shortsightedness of the fishermen thinking to keep up the price of coral, or the want of knowledge in the use of the apparatus, we cannot tell ; but in the cases where diving apparatus has been supplied the owners have spoken of their great success in obtaining pure specimens in all colours, from the pale pink to the dark red, and in some cases black, and we believe they have not complained either in the commercial point of view. Amber is found in the Baltic, on the coast of Prussia, in tolerable quantities, but as yet the use of the diving apparatus has not formed any important industry. We hope when the attention of practical men has been brought to this fishery, like those already mentioned, the diving apparatus will be the only means of obtaining this important resinous exudation of an extinct genus of coniferous trees from the depths of the sea.

ROMAN AMPHORA WITH SPONGE ADHERING.
(Recovered off the coast of Rhodes in 1875. Probable age 200 B.C.)

HOW TO DIVE.

Here are a few hints which Mr. Gorman gives to divers :—With inexperienced men it is advisable to have a rope ladder down to the bottom, but an expert diver prefers simply a rope ; they must both be weighted at the bottom. Each diver while under water requires a signalman to hold his life-line and air-pipe, both of which should be kept just taut, clear of the gunnel, so that any movement of the diver may be felt. The diver should descend slowly, halting for a few minutes after his head is under water, to satisfy himself that everything is correct, and then continue the descent. If he feels oppressed or experiences any humming noise in his ears, he should rise a yard or two and swallow his saliva several times; he must not continue to descend unless he feels comfortable. If oppression, singing in the ears, or headache continue, he must not persevere, but return slowly to the surface. To dive to great depths, such as 130 or 150 feet, requires men of great practice and able to sustain the consequen enormous pressure. On arriving at the bottom the diver will give one pull on the life-line to notify that he is "all right." In returning from great depths the diver should ascend very slowly, and thus avoid the effects of passing too abruptly from considerable pressure to that of the open air; if he stops now and then he gets gradually and regularly accustomed to the change. The ascent from the depth of twenty fathoms should occupy about five minutes. "It is more important to move slowly in rising than in descending." The diver takes down with him the ladder line, which he secures to the foot of the ladder or rope by which he has descended; this line should be coiled up in his hand with a loop round his wrist, and as he leaves the ladder he lets the line gradually uncoil, so that if he be at any distance off he can find his way back to the ladder when he wants to return. If working in thick water, while at the bottom, he should never let go the ladder

THE DIVER WRITING IN THE DEEP.

line: if by any accident he does so, and cannot find the latter, he must make the signal to be hauled up.

A FAMOUS DIVER.

Mr. Lambert, who has charge of the exhibit at Chelsea, is a famous diver. For fifteen years he was at sea, as apprentice and officer. "The sea is the best training for a boy," says Mr. Lambert. Mr. Lambert turned diver in 1866, and since then has visited every part of the globe, and has risked his life in many daring adventures. One of the most notable of these was the recovery of treasure from the

mail steamer, the *Alfhenso XII.*, which went down off Point Gando, Grand Canary, in 160 feet of water. She had on board treasure valued at £100,000. The underwriters who had insured this treasure organised a salvage expedition, which was despatched to the scene of the wreck. A short time afterwards a telegram was received from the captain of the steamer as follows:—"Lambert has got both scuttles open, and has got into the magazine. The boxes of gold are there." The treasure-room was in the run of the ship with three decks above it, at a depth of 26¼ fathoms, so that the task of salving was an unprecedented one. The operations were persevered in, in the face of unforeseen difficulties and complications, and at last £70,000 was rescued from the deep. This was one of Mr. Lambert's greatest feats. After the wreck had been discovered the steamer was moored to buoys almost over it, and the divers were able to lower themselves on to the top of the mizen mast, and then slide down on to the deck. Mr. Lambert blew up a portion of the deck, and descended to the bullion-room through the wreckage, remaining down as long as twenty and thirty minutes at this enormous depth. He wears one of the rescued dollars on his watch-chain.

THE SEVERN TUNNEL.

The boldest of Mr. Lambert's feats was his descent of the shaft leading to the workings of the Severn Tunnel. The workings were flooded, the men standing idle: it was necessary to shut an iron-door through which the water was rushing at a tremendous rate into the main tunnel. It was a journey of a quarter of a mile through a baby tunnel, about eight feet high by as many wide. The baby tunnel was blocked with *débris*, which were swirling about in a dark underground torrent. With a dress which was self-feeding, which had never been practically tried; without air-pipe, without life-line:

relying upon the little store of oxygen in the reservoir, this brave man descended the shaft, crowbar in hand, and made his way through the black stream to the iron door through which the water was rushing. Two rails had to be prized up before he could attempt to close the door. He got one up, and then, after being two hours away, returned to the mouth of the pit, thinking that the oxygen was nearly exhausted. There was just enough left to last twenty minutes. A second supply came down from London, and a second time Lambert descended, and succeeded in shutting the door, and thus stopped the flooding of the mine.

The other thing of most interest in the Camperdown Gallery is the Torpedo Exhibit. We give below a sketch of one of the model tanks in the Gallery, which is fitted up so as to show the use of mines and torpedo attack. First, however, it may be well to give a word of general explanation. "A torpedo may be defined," says Mr. Laird Clowes in his little book, "All About the Royal Navy," "as an explosive case, which may be fired either automatically by concussion, or at the will of the user, and which is stationary under water or travels through the water. Some travelling torpedos are moved by being towed, others by the working of independent machinery concealed within them, others by being carried at a boat's bow, or pushed ; and yet others by a controlling power

NAVAL DIVERS.

worked from the shore or from some other fixed station. The object of a torpedo is primarily to attack and blow up a hostile vessel ; but torpedoes are also designed for clearing channels, and for destroying other torpedoes—especially those stationary torpedoes which are usually known as mines. The forms of torpedo principally used in the British service are four in number :—Fixed torpedoes, or mines ; spar torpedoes, or explosive cases carried at the end of a spar at a boat's bow ; automobile torpedoes, such as the Whitehead and Schwartzkopf ; and controllable torpedoes, such as the Brennan. The exploding material may be either gunpowder or one of the compounds which are known as 'high explosives.' The method of exploding is by concussion or electric contact, or by means of a current sent along a wire from an operator at a post of observation." In the model tank sketched below, on the extreme left is the attacking force, and in the right corner is the defending ironclad. Various submarine mines in the harbour are also shown. In the middle of the sketch is a torpedo boat in the act of lifting itself over the boom which is supposed to protect the defending ironclad ; while the three sketches at the top of the next page explain the action of the second torpedo boat. The object in attacking with this form of torpedo is to approach the ship without being observed, and to explode the gun-cotton at the end of

THE MINING MODEL.

the pole in actual contact with the ship's side. The next two sketches show, first, the attaching of an explosive to a ship's cable; and, second, the effect

thereof. The defending mines shown in the model of the harbour are fired from the ironclad.

THE TORPEDO BREAKS THE CABLE.

THE DIVER FIXES THE TORPEDO TO THE CABLE.

TORPEDO STEAM PINNACE.

A TORPEDO MINE EXPLODED.

CHAPTER XIV.

THE ARMSTRONG GALLERY.

UNMISTAKABLY the most important, and perhaps also the most interesting, exhibit at the Naval Exhibition is the Armstrong collection of ships' guns and ships' models, in which the visitor finds himself after leaving the Camperdown Gallery. Whatever may have been the case a few years ago, it is probably unnecessary at this time of day to enlarge upon the standing and capacity of what we have before ventured to describe as "Britain's supplementary Arsenal" at Elswick-on-Tyne. It is certainly the most varied and extensive institution of the kind, public or private, in this country or abroad—for, remember it is not, like the public works at Woolwich, or the semi-public works at Essen, a gun-factory merely: the steel out of which the guns are made is turned out in great ingots in furnaces and forging-presses adjoining the gun-shops; the ordnance works (which occupy forty acres, contain upwards of 800 machines, and employ some 3,500 hands) provide not only guns, but the carriages upon which they have to be worked, and the projectiles required to make them effective weapons of destruction; and, finally, berths for the building of ships of war of the most powerful types are provided in a yard to the east of the gun-shops and immediately below the steel-works. In brief, as Messrs. Armstrong, Mitchell, & Co. justly boast, Elswick (where 16,500 men were employed last summer, as against 14,000 at Woolwich) is the only factory in the world, national or private, that can build a man-of-war and arm her completely. With this preface, we will glance at the exhibits, which include a representation of "the battery-deck of a modern armour-clad" and a turret containing a 110-ton gun.

How Gun-Steel is Tested.

The sight of several cylinders of steel lying in the neighbourhood of the 110-ton gun, however, induces us to essay, first, the task of outlining the processes which evolve out of the rough ingot the exact and beautifully finished gun. At the steel works at Elswick—which include in their design four 25-ton Siemens's furnaces and one 40-ton furnace, and one 3,000-ton, one 4,000-ton, and one 6,000-ton forging-press—ingots of a very large size are produced. In many cases these ingots are solid, and for gun-purposes have to be bored out as hereafter described; but it is gradually becoming the custom especially in the case of ingots intended for the largest class of guns, to cast and forge them hollow. The tensile strength of the ingots varies from 26 tons to the square inch, with 27 per cent. of ductility, up to 32 tons per square inch with 15 per cent. of ductility, oil hardened. To avoid the internal strain caused by the irregular or too rapid cooling, the ingots after leaving the mould are placed in a huge pit, where, simply covered with ashes, they cool slowly and evenly. For, be it carefully noted, gun-steel is subjected in this country to the severest tests, both private and official. First a disc is sawn off each end; and out of each of these discs there are cut four testing pieces about three inches long, with heads resembling short double-headed bolts. These test-pieces having been hardened at a temperature of about 1,500 deg. Fahr., are seized at either end in the jaws of a testing-machine (not larger than a copying-press, but as powerful as a locomotive and pulled apart by hydraulic pressure. Those conducting the tests have first to note when the steel commences to yield as it begins to elongate under the strain to which it is subjected, and next to elongate a piece until a point is reached when the steel ceases to return after expansion to its original length. A self-registering apparatus is attached to the machine to ensure perfect accuracy. Finally, the breaking-strain is ascertained by adding weight until a test-piece breaks. Take a bolt tested while we look on: The first test shows that the steel began

LORD ARMSTRONG.

D

to move at a pressure of 15 tons to the square inch; the second proves that the amount of the strain which the steel will stand without permanent set is 21 tons per square inch—in the bolt two inches long the measure of elongation is found to be just under half an inch; and the third shows that it breaks at 36·3 tons per square inch. In the case of the 110-ton gun, the minimum requirements of the War-Office when the steel is in a soft state, fresh from the steel-works, are these: yielding strain, 11 to 15 tons to the square inch: amount of elongation above 15 per cent. of the length tested; and breaking strain between 27 and 35 tons per square inch. Similar tests, with other bolts, follow upon the ingot being hardened by heat and tempered by being plunged into oil. At this last series of tests the minimum requirement for a 110-ton gun are these: Yielding strain, 25 to 33 tons to the square inch; amount of elongation, above 10 per cent. of the length tested; and breaking strain, 34 to 46 tons per square inch. The division of the 110-ton gun into forty-four sections entails a really enormous number of tests—thus: the barrel is credited with twelve tests for each end—24; the other 43 pieces have four test pieces taken from each end—344. Thus the total number of tests made in the case of each 110-ton gun is 368: No less than 92 pieces of steel are prepared for the test, even for a small gun such as the 4·7-inch: and as the cost of preparing each test piece cannot possibly be taken as less than 10s., it will be seen that this process alone costs, for the 4·7-inch gun, £45. 10s. In the case of the largest guns the preparation of the test pieces actually entails a loss of 6½ tons of steel!

How a Gun is Built.

The introduction of slow-burning powder and minor causes have led to some change in the last few years in the form of our guns; the chamber in which the charge was stored, which was often several inches wider than the barrel, has been minimised and the barrel has been lengthened several feet. But the manner of building guns has not undergone material alteration. An Armstrong gun consists of a barrel covered with steel hoops, or cylinders, shrunk on to give necessary strength to the structure; thus at the breech end there may be as many as three "courses" or layers of cylinders or hoops, and at the muzzle end there is probably only one such course over the barrel. In other words, a gun is really a succession of cylinders of steel shrunk over each other. Expanded by the application of heat, the outside cylinder or "jacket," although its bore has been made slightly less than the outside diameter of the cylinder which it has to cover, is easily slipped over the inner tube; and as it gradually cools, the "jacket" grips with great power the inside cylinder. The grip of the cylinders upon each other grows in severity as the outside of the gun is reached,

and the compression upon the original cylinder, of course, increases with each layer added. This fact discloses the application of an important principle in gun-making—at any rate, as practised at Elswick. In a natural way, the great strain following upon the explosion of the charge of powder would fall heaviest upon the inner cylinder (or barrel) in which the explosion takes place, and the outer cylinders would only experience it in a diminishing degree; so that there would be a point under such circumstances where thickness ceased to add strength. This state of things is reversed at Elswick; the exterior parts prove the salvation of the gun. If the gun were made out of one piece of steel, as we have said, the strain of the explosion would not travel far beyond the bore—the exterior parts would be so much useless metal; but by the subdivision of the gun into cylinders, each cylinder, having been put into a high state of tension by being shrunk on, brings the full measure of its power to withstand strain to the support of the inner cylinder, or bore, and the other parts of the gun—that is, each successive layer reinforces the accumulated resisting power of the whole mass. A further consequence of the system of shrinking the cylinders one over the other is that the compression experienced by the original cylinder or barrel is so extreme that the outer cylinders, owing to their being, on the contrary, in a state of tension, first take the strain created by the explosion, and as the outer cylinders expand or extend (as the quality of metal guarantees that they will do, in a large degree, under the force of pressure), the strain is progressively imparted to the original tube; which ultimately receives its allotted proportion. The amount of compression exercised by the whole of the layers, when the gun is built up, is sufficient to reduce the internal diameter in the case of a 110-ton gun by 0.03 inches. Every part of the gun is thus made to bear a uniform share of the work.

The Boring and "Jacketing" of a Gun.

The tests having proved the sufficiency of the metal, the boring of the barrel, and the outer cylinder or "jacket" is begun. Let us take the fortune of a barrel—say the barrel of a 12-inch 43-ton gun which we followed under the boring operation at Elswick. First, it is "rough-bored," then "fine-bored," and lastly, "fine-turned," of course, where an ingot has been forged hollow the "rough-bore" is saved. The "rough-bore" is a heavy piece of work. The ingot cylinder of steel, lying longitudinally upon substantial supports, has an outside diameter of 21 in., and a circular cutter is at work in the centre, cutting out metal to the extent of 9½ in. With the barrel 30 ft. long, the rough boring occupies more than a week, although the machines (like most of the machines in the Elswick shops) work both day and night. The bore or cutter, which is carried on the end of a sub-

THE BATTERY DECK OF A MODERN ARMOUR-CLAD.

THE MODEL OF THE 110-TON GUN.

stantial shaft, advances at the rate of $4\frac{3}{4}$ in. per hour, assuming it could be kept at work continuously, but as a matter of fact it is frequently withdrawn to admit of the examination of the bore and ensure the accuracy of the "cut." Although it has behind it a powerful pressure, the bore travels silently and with singular slowness. The slightest irregularity in its progress over any part of the cylinder might easily mean the complete ruin of the ingot. Having been rough-bored, the barrel is toughened by being heated and tempered by being dipped in a pit of oil, operations all managed by means of hydraulic cranes. Then comes the process called "fine-boring." This is a very short, easy descriptive phrase; but with the largest guns it sometimes means, we are told, two to three months' work. It, in fact, comprises three separate borings. In the case of the 43-ton gun, the rough "cuts" in this stage take two or three weeks each. With the 110-ton gun, a "pass" or "cut" at the same stage occupies from three to four weeks. In the final boring from 700th to 1-10th of an inch, according to the gun, is left to be taken out. This operation requires the greatest care. If the bore becomes torn or damaged by the breaking of a tool or seizure of the boring head, a barrel which may now be worth between £2,000 and £3,000 is utterly spoiled; but happily this occurs very rarely. Each cylinder has to be treated in almost exactly the same fashion as the barrel or central tube, that is, each cylinder has to be tested, turned, rough and fine "bored," and gauged carefully throughout, to ensure correctness of diameter. The difficulties attending the attainment of accuracy of all these borings are great, particularly in the case of the barrel, for as the cutter of the bore wears down as it approaches the end of the cylinder, the diameter of the tube diminishes—thus : 30.75, 30.74. The barrel having been turned in the lathe on the outside is ready to receive its "jackets." The 43-ton gun had four "jackets" —that is, it was made of five cylinders, including the barrel. These cylinders ran in thickness thus : barrel, $4\frac{3}{4}$ in.; second course, 5 in.; third course, $3\frac{1}{4}$ in.; fourth course, $3\frac{1}{2}$ in.; fifth course, $4\frac{3}{4}$ in. The gun was thickest over the powder chamber—about $19\frac{1}{4}$ in.—of course, because it is the seat of the explosion. In the guns made for our national service the barrel is uncovered to the extent of 8 ft. from the muzzle, but in the 10-inch guns made at Elswick the second course is carried right up to the muzzle, and the old-fashioned swell at the muzzle is coming again in vogue. As all these cylinders except the inmost one are in short lengths, the 110-ton gun comprises no less than forty-four pieces, apart from the breech screw and the mechanism for closing it. When the gun is being built up, it stands in a pit, where the cylinder "jacket" next to be placed upon it is brought by a hydraulic lift from one of a series of furnaces heated by gas 'made in gas producers) and dropped over it. With a shield over it, it then gradually cools.

THE RIFLING AND FINISHING OF THE GUN.

Then comes the rifling of the gun. This has been postponed until all the cylinders are on, because of the unevenness in the interior of the barrel which the varying thicknesses of the cylinders create, which has to be ground out before the rifling can commence. The cutter is directed on its twisted movements by a pinion and rack, which in their turn are acted upon by wheels rolling along a slightly curved track or framework of iron. The cutter appears to travel along the barrel at a quicker rate than does the boring bar when a gun is being bored; but although the rifling only extends up four-fifths of the length of the gun, the operation in the case of a 43-ton gun occupies over a week, with the machine working double shift. The rifling of a 110-ton gun, with a barrel 42 feet in length, takes a month. The pitch of the rifling is progressive, and with a 43-ton gun the cutter will make one turn in every 45 feet. The cutter—which only cuts in coming out—goes up each groove from eight to twelve times, according to the hardness of the metal, and, as there are eighty grooves in many instances it travels along the gun eight hundred times. The greatest conceivable care has to be exercised in the rifling of these huge guns, as the slightest departure from the true course may now destroy material and work worth together £15,000. Two to four-hundredths of an inch are cut out in the rifling. The difference between the weight of a finished gun and the weight of the metal taken for its construction ranges from 40 to 50 per cent. The gun is "chambered" and fitted with the "breech screw" at such times as may prove most convenient. As is specially exemplified in the 4·7 quick-firing gun on exhibition—where the screw is made of a coned instead of a cylindrical shape—the breech-piece—i.e., the swinging gate of the gun—is now a wonderful and beautiful piece of mechanism. It is scarcely possible to conceive of greater simplicity with greater security : it opens and locks with the fewest conceivable number of motions apparently; and the gun cannot possibly be fired until everything is in the most perfect order. The ingenious arrangement for the prevention of the escape of the powder gases—a most important factor, inasmuch as in the 110-ton gun the charge of 960 lb. will give a pressure of gas equal to about 15 tons per square inch—also demands notice. While they can on occasion be fired mechanically, the large guns are now all fired by electrical apparatus, small batteries being attached to the guns and, as we have indicated, the gun cannot be fired until there is mechanical indication and permission, for, unless several levers each lie in a particular way, it is impossible for the electric circuit to be completed. In all these respects the gun of to-day is in most striking contrast to the first gun constructed by Lord (then Mr. William) Armstrong—a national curiosity, which stands modestly under the shadow of the model of the monster 110-ton gun.

WHAT IS DUE TO THE NEW SLOW-BURNING POWDER.

Guns, as we have indicated, have lately been built longer in order to get the full advantage of the slow-burning powder which is now being used. This combination of longer gun and slower powder gives a higher velocity, which means in effect not only a longer range, but also greater penetrative power and destructive energy on the part of the shot. With the old powder the shot received merely a sharp, short blow—that is to say, the powder suddenly produced a very high pressure, which fell immediately the shot commenced its movement—and had a long gun been employed, the result would really have been a dimi-

Committee on Explosives, a velocity of no less than 2,669 ft. has been realised with a 194-lb. charge of cordite from a 6-inch quick-firing gun. The service pressure put upon the chambers of the gun, it may be noted here, is 15 tons per square inch, which is more than three hundred times as high a pressure as that of a locomotive boiler.

THE BATTERY-DECK OF A MODERN MAN-OF-WAR.

Now that we have got an impression how guns—especially big guns—are constructed, we can the more harmoniously and profitably realise the striking piece of "realism" in the shape of the battery-deck and turrets of a modern man-of-war, for which the Executive Council of the Exhibition are indebted

MESSRS. ARMSTRONG'S WORKSHOPS : GUNS AWAITING INSPECTION.

nution of velocity. With the new slow-burning powder, a high pressure in the bore can be maintained for a much longer period, with the advantages already described. With this modern powder, the rates at which projectiles emitted from the most powerful armour-piercing guns will travel may be taken at from 2,000 ft. to 2,100 ft. per second, as compared with 1,400 ft. per second at the time the Government appointed the Committee on Explosives. But in the judgment of Captain Noble, C.B., F.R.S., the eminent authority on guns and explosives, who has for many years been Lord Armstrong's chief lieutenant, "we are not at all at the end of progress". With " amide " powder nearly 2,500 ft. velocity has already been obtained ; from a six-inch gun with the new explosive called " cordite," recommended by the

to the good-will and enterprise of Messrs. Armstrong, Mitchell & Co., who must have incurred considerable cost in the undertaking. " The battery-deck of a modern man-of-war " first attracts us. The main armament here consists of three 4·7 quick-firing guns and a couple of 6-pounder Hotchkiss guns. In between these stand the mess-tables, with the mess-lockers above, and the mess-cans and biscuit kit near at hand, with a huge kitchener, capable of cooking for upwards of 500 men, in the centre of the deck. There are a couple of stand of Martini rifles at the end of the deck, together with the cutlasses and revolvers for use in boarding and for defence in the last resort. In front of each gun, it may also be noted, there are suspended from the rafters cutlasses and boarding-pikes sufficient for a •

battery, available for use whenever boarding parties should be in demand. At the end will be found specimens of officers' cabins. These cabins, having been prettily and more than adequately furnished, prove a great popular attraction. The eye here takes in many things, and the mind is curious about several. Why, for instance, so many pairs of boots? Well, your naval officer likes to be prepared for all climates, for all weathers, and for all kinds of entertainments and functions. Note the tennis-bats and cricket-bats, the dumb-bells, the boxing-gloves, the fencing paraphernalia—all suggesting that our lieutenants and captains of to-day are determined that it shall not be said of them, should fame await them, that they lacked any of the graces which came of a

east corner, which does not call for special remark. The type of gun most prominent here—the 4.7 gun —is at present one of the strongest cards in the pack of the Elswick firm, which is greatly enamoured of it, as indeed is our own Government. It is, in fact, the pattern of gun which now forms the main armament of all our first-class cruisers, and it was chiefly designed to repel the attack of torpedo boats. The type found its first success in the fact that the 4.7 45-pounder gun could do in 47 seconds what it took the 5-inch B.L. gun five minutes to perform. It is capable of firing twelve shots a minute; and assuming a war-vessel to be armed with a broadside of three of these guns, a torpedo boat would run seventy-two chances of being hit in the two

A NAVAL LIEUTENANT'S HOME.

carefully-trained physique. The visitor is scarcely likely to miss the array of portraits of beauties of the stage, especially as the significance of the display is emphasized by the text arranged above it, "Husbands love your wives" (Col. iii. 19 : a sly joke at the alleged weaknesses of our brave defenders, at which many people roar and a few are indignant. Altogether, these cabins form a bright little picture, casting the life of the officers of "the Queen's Navee" into a more tempting frame than has in the eyes of the mere "land-lubber" hitherto enclosed it.

THE QUICK-FIRING GUNS.

Now let us glance at the guns which line the battery-deck, with the exception of the gun at the

minutes she would spend in speeding over the 1,300 yards she would probably need to traverse to begin her attack. By the way, artillerists, it seems, agree that a rate of about ten rounds a minute is sufficient for all guns larger than the 6-pounder; any quicker rate is liable to be obtained at the cost of impaired efficiency in other directions, and carelessness on the part of the crew in loading and aiming. A later gun of the same pattern as the 4.7 gun before us is a 6-inch gun to fire projectiles of 100 lbs. The Admiralty put this gun to severe and prolonged tests little more than six months ago at Silloth, the First Lord of the Admiralty himself attending the trials; in fact, from one gun and mounting 260 rounds were fired before the Admiralty decided on

DISAPPEARING GUN : AT REST.

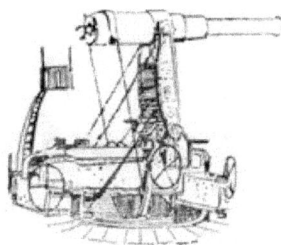

DISAPPEARING GUN : IN ACTION.

its acceptance—a test probably without precedent. At one of the trials ten rounds were fired at a target in 1 min. 31 sec. The latest gun is now to form the main armament of all our first-class cruisers. The weight of the gun here shown—the 4.7 gun—is 41 cwt.; the later gun of this same pattern—not here shown—weighs upwards of 5 tons. One of the vital elements accounting for the success of these quick-firing guns is the carriage on which it is mounted, which is of a novel and special character. Any description of this carriage, which is known as the "Elswick Mounting," would, we are afraid, be too technical to permit of a popular conception; but, in brief, it provides for the gun, by the absorption of its recoil

6-INCH QUICK-FIRING GUN : BLUE JACKETS LOADING.

energy, returning instantly after discharge to the loading position. The gun can be elevated or depressed or swung round to almost any degree, and the arrangements for training and firing appear to reach the acme of simplicity. Usually one man opens and closes the breech, a second man puts in the full cartridge and catches the empty case as it is ejected, a third man puts in the shot, and a fourth trains and fires the gun. Elevation is given by means of a hand-wheel, which gears into the elevating arc fitted on to the cradle, and this hand-wheel is so placed that it can be used with the left hand while the eye is on the sight, the right hand on the firing pistol, and the left shoulder pressed against the shoulder-

QUICK-FIRING GUN, FIRING ORDINARY POWDER.

QUICK-FIRING GUN, FIRING SMOKELESS POWDER.
(Cordite).

TARGET FIRED AT *BY THE* **110 TON ELSWICK BREECH LOADING GUN** *March 1879.*

← 11 FEET →
Concrete

← 5 FEET →
Granite

piece. Thus one man can train, elevate, and fire, without moving his eye from the sights. Even if the training-gear should be thrown out of working power, the gun can be trained solely by the shoulder-piece.

THE FIRING ARRANGEMENTS.

The firing arrangements, too, are very noticeable. The brass cartridge-cases which stand in front of each gun are one of the principal features of the quick-firing system: they are known as metallic cartridges. When these are brought into use, the electric wire is brought into contact with the electric primer at the centre of the outstanding brass stopper. You may here examine a solid drawn cartridge-case for the 4·7-inch gun which has been fired twenty times, and a built-up case for the 6-inch gun which has been fired sixteen times. The use of electric primers instead of the old-fashioned percussion primers in the cartridge-cases of course obviates all dangers of explosion. The 4·7-inch gun takes a projectile weighing 45 lbs., and the 6-inch gun one weighing 100 lbs. To obviate mishap in the electric firing arrangements, electric batteries, as will be noticed, are provided in duplicate, and sometimes even in triplicate. An electric sounder, too, is so arranged that it commences to ring, if everything is correct, directly the gun is loaded and in the firing position. As we have before explained, also, the gun can never be fired unless every mechanical feature of the breech and firing arrangements are in the most perfect juxtaposition. Should the electric arrangements fail, resort can be had in an easy fashion to ordinary percussion firing, although then, of course, the loading is not effected so rapidly.

THE HOTCHKISS GUN.

The smaller Hotchkiss quick-firing guns, which stand in between the 4·7 guns, are a better known weapon. These guns are mainly meant for use against on-coming torpedo boats, and they are generally scattered all over the ship, even in the tops and particularly in the stern, which is the weakest part from the torpedo-boat point of view. The single cylinder of steel of which it consists has a bore of 2⅜ in., and it weighs only 800 lbs. The carriage is on the recoil principle, and the gun is managed by three men. The gun, which takes a metallic cartridge, fires a shell weighing 6 lb. with a velocity of 1,820 ft. per second, and an energy of 137 ft.-tons. From this 6-pounder about twenty-five aimed shots can be fired per minute; and with a smaller form, the 3-pounder, about thirty aimed shots per minute can be discharged.

THE SHOOTING GALLERY.

Visitors are permitted to try both the 4·7 and the Hotchkiss 6-pounder, Messrs. Morris having obtained permission to use their tubes with a couple of the guns. In short, a shooting gallery for practice with these types of naval artillery—with pellets the size of peas as shots, and a target representing a torpedo-boat steaming at sea—exists in the immediate neighbourhood of "the battery-deck" which we are supposed to be inspecting.

THE "DISAPPEARING GUN" FOR COAST DEFENCE.

"Are forts going out of fashion?" is the question which rises to the lips when in the vicinity of the battery-deck we spy the "pit" in which the "Disappearing Gun" is on exhibition. Certainly, the scheme ought to commend itself to economists of

TARGET FIRED AT *BY THE* 110 TON ELSWICK BREECH-LOADING GUN *in* 1891.

20 FEET Clear

8 *in* × 20 *ins.* →

the Joseph Hume type. The gun is represented as in a pit, say a quarter of a mile from the shore, with the magazines behind it, also underground ; and it can be trained and fired, and, what is more, do much mischief, without any one of the gunners putting his head above ground, or the gun itself running great risk of hurt. It will be approximately trained and laid for elevation by means of reflecting sights— mirrors placed on the right-hand stanchion of the gun, one above and the other below the level of the barrel. The carriage is worked on the hydro-pneumatic system—that is, compressed air acts upon water. Theoretically, the air once inclosed in the air-chamber is supposed to last for ever, but leaks inevitably occur ; however, a few strokes once a month from a hand pump which forms an auxiliary to the gun suffices to fill the void. *Inter alia*, you may note lying about the gallery little flasks charged with air, which seem to be as much an accessory to the man-of-war on a campaign as a liquor-flask to a traveller on a long journey. The gun, which is a 5-ton 6-inch gun, is hoisted into firing position by a hydraulic cylindrical press, and after being fired returns to the loading position (and so drops out of sight) by the utilisation of its own recoil energy.

A HAND-WORKED GUN FOR CRUISERS.

Before we pass from the battery-deck to the turret we glance at a specimen of a hand-worked gun now in use in the Navy—notably in the *Impérieuse*— which is to be seen at the east end of the collection. It is a 9·2-inch gun on a Vavasseur mounting. The ammunition comes up a hoist through a tube fixed in the centre of the mounting, so that the gun can be loaded when it is in any position of training, and the gun and gunners are well protected by shields. Every operation can be performed by one man. Guns of this pattern are now being supplied for all our first-class cruisers.

THE 110-TON GUN.

Finally, we pass up into the turret—say the turret of her Majesty's ship *Victoria*, wherein is mounted a model of the 110-ton gun. Perhaps in view of the sundry stick-taps on the part of the visitors, it may be necessary to explain that both are models made of wood. Of course, we see only half the turret ; the other half and the second 110-ton gun are to be provided by the imagination. The turret is 27 ft. in height, and has an inside area of 600 ft. Taking the turret alone, there are usually four men in attendance on each gun—say, eight in the turret altogether. The primary portion of the turret is iron-girder work, which is covered with teak, and armoured to the depth of 17 inches. The heavy steel grating which covers the barrel of the gun is as much to let out the smoke as to admit the light. The turret of itself weighs 850 tons. Having examined the turret, let us turn to the mounting of this great gun. The pivot of the whole is the hydraulic press so inseparably identified with the name of Armstrong. The gun has no trunnions, but is strapped down to a carriage or "saddle," which rests on two long steel beams called "slides." The slides pivot so far forward as practicable, so that the centre, about which the gun moves for elevation or depression, may be as near the gun port-holes as possible, and the latter thus reduced to the smallest dimensions. This is exceedingly necessary for two reasons—first, so that the gun and crew may not be exposed to hostile bullets from machine-guns, entering through the port ; and, secondly, so that the opening for the sea to enter, if the ship is being fought in bad weather, may be reduced to the lowest limits. The saddle on which the gun rests is attached to a large piston rod entering the hydraulic press fixed between the slides, which hydraulic press serves for running the gun in and out as well as for absorbing the recoil. The huge stump-like elevating cylinders under the saddle will have on them always a weight of 73 tons each, the gun and its mounting by themselves weighing 146 tons ; but the two hydraulic presses under the slide, lift slide, saddle, gun, and recoil press without a jerk. The opening, loading, and closing of the gun is also performed by hydraulics, two separate presses being employed for this purpose. The fact that the breech screw weighs 39 cwt. is a sufficient proof that manual power cannot cope with such immense guns.

WHAT IF ITS MACHINERY SHOULD FAIL?

"What if the hydraulic machinery should go wrong?—wouldn't you be left with a very Jumbo in the way of white elephants?" is a bugbear often raised by the opponents of these big guns. But we have the assurance of Lord Armstrong's representatives, who, after all, are the most experienced and authoritative witnesses on the point, seeing that their firm has been identified from its initiation with the hydraulic principle, that hydraulic machinery rarely goes wrong. Even after a quarter of a century of work, machinery of that type has been found in a perfectly dependable state, and as a matter of fact in business transactions only 2½ per cent. is allowed for depreciation of hydraulic machinery. Visitors are invited to compare the breech arrangements of the 110-ton gun with those of the 9·2-inch 22-ton gun, when, say the firm, they will see that the hydraulic-worked arrangements of the great gun are much simpler than the hand-worked gear at the breech of the smaller gun. In the original armament of the *Thunderer* there were two 35-ton guns worked by hand, and two 38-ton guns worked by hydraulic power. The guns worked by hand required a crew of forty-two men, while a crew of only twenty-eight was sufficient for the guns mounted on the hydraulic system. As to reliability, the example of the *Téméraire* is also quoted by Messrs. Armstrong : the vessel has now been fourteen years in commission, and during the whole of that time her hydraulic machinery, which lacks many of the more modern simplifications, has never given the slightest trouble.

THE FIRING OF THE 110-TON GUN.

Now we will assume that this great gun is on the point of being fired with a full charge. The 110-ton gun, indeed all large guns, is fired with slow-burning

cocoa-powder—"cocoa" because of its brown colour. As you may observe in the powder case in the gallery, it is shaped in hexagonal prisms, this being the most convenient form for close packing. Each prism is pierced with a hole in the centre, so as to give ready access to the flame and insure an equable ignition. Ten thousand of these prisms are needed to make up a full charge for this monster gun ! The powder, along with the shell, comes up from the magazine below in a hoist (indicated at the rear of model), and, having been placed on a spout-tray, is rammed into the gun by a hydraulic rammer (also indicated at the rear of the model), the shell, of course, having been first driven forward into its place by the same instrument. In nearly all naval guns the powder charge is made up into four cartridges, the object being to get each cartridge down to a weight that a man may lift. But on account of its extraordinary weight—960 lbs. :—the charge for the 110-ton gun is divided into eight cartridges. Specimens of these cartridges, to the extent of the full charge, stand as a pyramid close to the hoist. The material of the envelope, by the way, is silk cloth. At the back of each envelope, next to the primer, there stand a few prisms of black powder, because it more readily ignites than the cocoa powder. Each of these eight cartridges weighs 120 lbs. To load, it is necessary to bring the gun in at extreme elevation, and then the following operations are gone through :—

1. Unlock and un-screw the breech-lock.
2. Withdraw breech-block.
3. Traverse breech-blocks to one side.
4. Place the loading-tray in the gun.
5. Wash out the gun.
6. Ram home the projectile.
7. Ram home first half-charge.
8. Ram home second half-charge.
9. Withdraw loading-tray.
10. Traverse breech-screw.
11. Insert breech-screw.
12. Screw up and lock breech-screw.

The gun having been sighted by the captain of the turret from his conning-tower, is also fired by him by electricity. The gun can be loaded and fired within two and a half minutes.

THE SHOT AND ITS TERRIBLE HAVOC.

The projectile fired from the gun when attacking ships or forts weighs 1,800 lbs., and it goes out with a velocity of 2,105 ft. per second, and has a destructive energy equal to 33,305 foot-tons. If the gun need to be used against a body of men or a flotilla of boats, shrapnel shell would be used—that is, the long drum-like cylinder of steel standing close to the carriage would be shot from the gun, and its contents (2,300 4-oz. bullets) would scatter death amongst the foe. The bullets are put in in layers, though not with mathematical exactness—they are merely shaken together. Melted rosin is poured in among them, in order to fill up the interstices : else, when the heavy

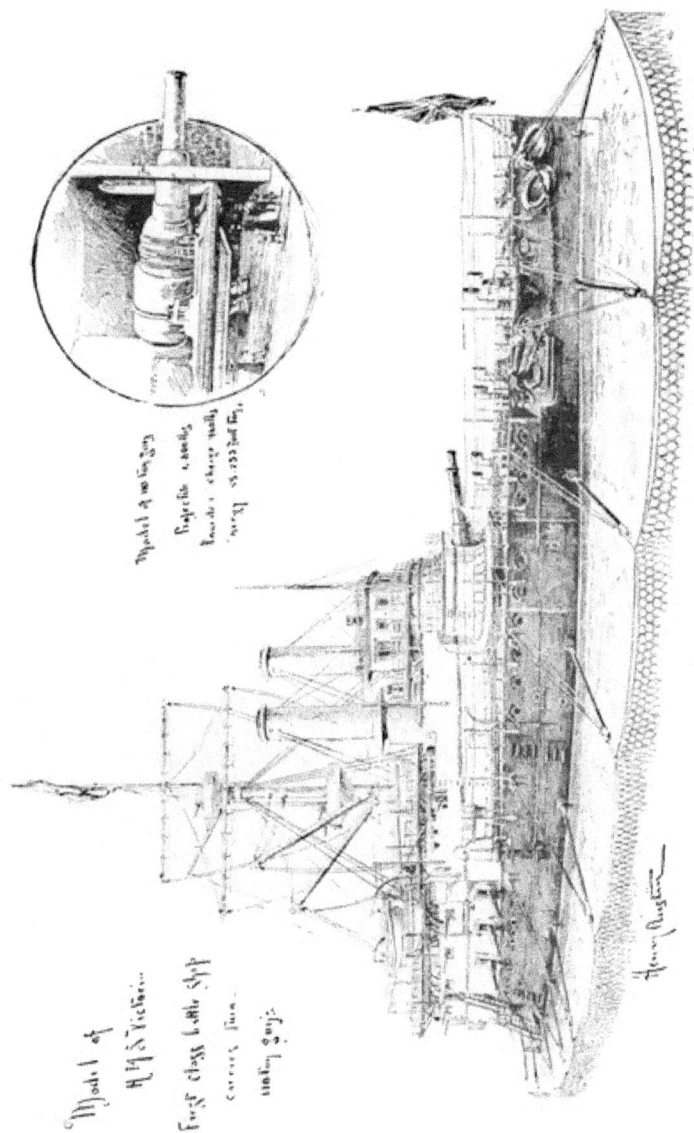

H.M.S. "VICTORIA."

Sister Ship to H.M.S. Sanspareil. First-class battle ship 10,470 ton : carrying 25 guns, including two 110-ton guns. 14,000 horse-power; twin screw.

shock of the explosion came they would be all flattened against each other. Directly the shrapnel case bursts, the bullets go flying on, while the spin of the shell, communicated by the rifling of the gun, spreads them out by centrifugal force over a large area. But the gun will most likely be used for attacking armoured ships and forts; in this case the steel shell, with a strong, sharp point, will be used. These shells are first forged, then bored, and finally tempered. While they should be tough in the body, they must be hard at the striking point. The hardness of the point increases the penetrative power of the shell, while the toughness of the body prevents it swelling as it is entering the plate and so increasing the difficulties of penetration. A good shell carries itself into the interior of the ship before it explodes. The shell is constructed to carry such an amount of powder as will cause it to explode and add its pieces to the destructive splinters from the broken plate. The shell used in this gun, as stated, weighs 1,800 lbs. The terrible havoc which such a shell will play when fired with a full charge from this gun is most vividly illustrated on the wall closest to the model. There is given a sketch of the course of the shell from the 110-ton gun of the *Sanspareil* at a trial at Shoeburyness in March last. The shell tore its way at the rate of 2,079 ft. per second through 20 in. of compound armour specially manufactured; 8 in. of iron fastened in a heavy wrought-iron frame; 20 ft. of oak baulks; 5 ft. of granite blocks; 11 ft. of concrete; and 6 ft. of brick; altogether, 44 ft. 4 in. of a wall unique in history, surely, for combination of width and variety and strength of material! Everybody should see this most graphic picture of the attainments, power, and tendencies of this our day and generation! For firing a full charge with armour-piercing shot from the 110-ton gun, the country pays—for the powder, £80; for the shell and fuses, £125—total, £200; not to mention a much more serious item if the gun were continually being fired with a full charge, the damage from the erosion caused by the powder gases, which causes it to lose its accuracy, and necessitates its being re-lined, at great expense and at the cost of long delay. It is generally considered, says Captain Noble, in the work already referred to, " Modern Naval Artillery," that the life of the 67-ton guns may be taken at 120 rounds, and the 110-ton gun at 75 rounds, both with full charges.

THE NEW SMOKELESS POWDER AND ITS EFFECT.

Before we pass from the guns, a few words on the new smokeless powder will not be out of place. The most promising of the new explosives, says Captain Noble, is cordite, though the climatic trials of it are not complete. As will be seen from the sample shown in the gallery above, it resembles long pieces of thin black or grey cord, and when placed in a gun, say in the metallic cartridge for use in the 4.7 or 6-inch gun, where the smokeless powder is essential, it is tied up like a bundle of sticks. We reproduce from Captain Noble's book instantaneous photographs, showing the contrast between the effects of the old and the new smokeless powder when the 6-inch gun has been fired (see p. 33). In the " Cordite' picture, what appears to be smoke is really almost entirely, it is stated, the dust and sand which were raised by the firing of the gun. With this new explosive, as high a velocity as 2,430 feet per second has been obtained in a 6-inch gun with moderate pressure.

A FINE COLLECTION OF NOTABLE MODELS.

In the gallery above we get an impressive notion of Messrs. Armstrong, Mitchell, & Co.'s achievements as shipbuilders and general engineers. Here may be seen a number of fine models. First we may point out a model of the Chilian ship *Esmeralda*, now attracting so much attention, which was built by the firm, and a model of the *Giovanni Bausan*, constructed for the Italian Government on practically the same lines. An advance upon these ships were two vessels built for the Japanese Government—the *Naniwa* and *Takachiho-kan*—the first two of a splendid series of progressively improving ships of war, designed for the firm by Mr. W. H. White, who was director of the shipbuilding department of the Armstrong Company before he was called to the distinguished post of Director of Naval Construction at the British Admiralty. There are here also two protected cruisers, built for the Chinese Government, the first of these being the *Chih Yuen*. We cannot pretend to catalogue the various models, even although these represent only a small proportion of the ships the Elswick firm has turned out. But, with our colonial sympathies, we must direct attention to the models of the *Katoomba*, one of five cruisers for the Australian colonies, and the *Boomerang*, one of two fast torpedo-boat destroyers. Photographs of these vessels have been given on pp. 20 and 21.

THE FASTEST CRUISER IN THE WORLD.

Now we may pass on to the most finished and interesting model in the gallery, bar one. This is a model of the fastest cruiser in the world—the 25 *de Mayo*, at this moment on the point of sailing from the Tyne. The 25 *de Mayo* has been built for the

Argentine Government, from designs by Mr. Philip Watts, the present chief constructor at Elswick. This model is on a scale which presents everything 1-48th of the actual size : and it took three men three months to make. Only the miniature stanchion posts that support the chains running round the after-deck were bought ; the chains themselves were made by a little boy. The decks are yellow pine ; the deck-houses of inlaid walnut ; the gratings of boxwood ; and the bulwarks are enamelled. Justice is done to every feature of the ship ; even the little cabins are fitted up as in the original.

THE CHAMPION MODEL.

But *the* triumph of the Gallery is the model of H.M.S. *Victoria*, the present flagship of the British squadron in the Mediterranean, which was launched at Elswick in 1887. The model represents the *Victoria* with her torpedo-nets down, and generally ready for action. It is on the extremely liberal scale of one inch to the foot, or one-twelfth full size. True, it is only a half model ; but by means of a mirror running the full length the public are presented with a picture of the complete vessel. The model has been constructed to represent the real ironclad in every minute detail. It is 34 ft. long and 5 ft. 6 in. broad from torpedo-net to torpedo-net. The decks are of yellow pine, the deck-houses of teak. The fittings are in every way in exact resemblance to the actual fittings : wire is represented by fine wire, cordage by cordage, albeit the finer kinds are made of silk : even in the torpedo-nets each ring is formed exactly in the same way as the original nets. Ten men were employed for four months in constructing the model, and the cost runs up to £2,000.

THE "VICTORY" AND THE "VICTORIA."

This notice will fitly conclude with a contrast between the two great V's—the *Victory* and the *Victoria*—for which we are indebted to Lord Armstrong and Captain Noble—(see the admirable work by Captain Noble, issued as a species of supplement to the Catalogue of the Exhibition). The *Victory* was a three-decker, 186 ft. in length, 52 ft. in breadth, with a displacement of 3,500 tons, and she carried an armament of 102 guns, consisting of thirty 42 and 32-pounders, thirty 24-pounders, forty 12-pounders, and two 68-pounder carronades (the heaviest of her guns was a 42-pounder), and she had a complement of nearly 900 men. With the exception of a few small brass guns, the guns were mere blocks of cast iron, he sole machining to which they were subjected consisting in the formation of the bore and the drilling of the vent. A large proportion of nearly every armament consisted of carronades—a piece which was in those days in great favour. They threw a shot of large diameter from a light gun with a low charge, and their popularity was chiefly due to the rapidity with which they could be worked. But as the great object of every English commander was, if it were possible, to bring his ship alongside that of the enemy, the low velocity given by the carronades became of comparatively small moment, while the ease of working and the large diameter of the shot were factors of the first importance.

The *Victoria* has a length of 340 ft., a breadth of 70 ft. ; she has a displacement of about 10,500 tons, an indicated horse-power of 14,244, and she attained a speed on the measured mile of 17½ knots ; she has a thickness of 17 in. of compound armour on her turrets, 18 in. protects the redoubt, and her battery-deck is defended with 3-in. plates. Her armament consists of two 16½-in. 110-ton guns, one 10-in. 30-ton gun, twelve 6-in. 5-ton guns, twelve 6-pounder and nine 3-pounder quick-firing guns, two machine-guns, and six torpedo-guns. While the heaviest gun on board the *Victory* was a little over 3 tons, the heaviest on board the *Victoria* is a little over 110 tons. The largest charge used on board the *Victory* was 10 lb., the largest on board the *Victoria* close on 1,000 lb. ; the heaviest shot used in the *Victory* was 68 lb., in the *Victoria* it is 1,800 lb. The weight of metal discharged from the broadside of the *Victory* was 1,150 lb., from that of the *Victoria* it is 4,750 lb. But, having regard to the energy of the broadside, the power of each ship is better indicated by the quantity of powder expended than by the weight of metal discharged, and, while the broadside fire from the *Victory* consumed only 355 lb. of powder, that from the *Victoria* consumes 3,120 lb. But it is when we come to the machinery involved in our first-rates that the contrast between the past and the present is brought most strongly into prominence. The *Victoria* has no less than eighty-eight engines. This number is exclusive of the machinery in the torpedo and other steamboats, and of the locomotive engines in the torpedoes carried, which are themselves engines of a most refined and delicate character. When the *Victory* fought the battle of Trafalgar she had been afloat for forty years, and her total cost, complete with her armament and all stores was probably considerably under £100,000. The cost of a first-rate man-of-war of the present day, similarly complete, would be nearly £1,000,000.

CHAPTER XV

THE ST. VINCENT GALLERY AND THE LAKE.

THE ORIGINAL MAXIM GUN.

ON leaving the Armstrong Gallery, the visitor will next enter the St. Vincent Gallery, which also is devoted to naval ordnance. The contents of the gallery will be found of great interest by technical men : but after the full account which we have given of guns and gun-making in the preceding chapter, we need not pursue the subject here in detail.

Special attention should, however, be called to the exhibits of the Maxim-Nordenfelt Gun Company. These include a number of quick-firing and machine guns, some of which are quite new—as, for instance, the " Maxim-Nordenfelt automatic quick-firer." " The operator," says a writer in the *Times*, "has only to pitch the cartridge into the open breech. All else is done for him. The rim of the cartridge case, as it passes, strikes two catches, which not only raise the breech-block behind the cartridge, but induce a sequence of motions that fire the charge, depress the breech-block again, eject the empty case, and make everything ready for a repetition of the whole proceeding." The Maxim automatic machine-gun is shown in two or three calibres, and in a little tent

outside the Armstrong Gallery there is one which the visitor may have fired for him on payment of 6*d.* The great principle of the Maxim gun is the utilisation of the recoil, by the use of which the weapon becomes a self-feeding and self-firing gun. The end of a canvas belt holding 333 cartridges (each about a quarter of an inch apart) having been inserted by hand into the breech from a box immediately below, the gun is started by pressing a button in front of the gunner or holding down a brass trigger immediately below the button. One shot having been fired, the recoil force cocks the hammer, draws the next cartridge into the barrel, locks the breech, pulls the trigger, and ejects the bullet out of the muzzle and the empty cartridge case out of an orifice below the breech ; and the gun goes on disposing of cartridge after cartridge in like manner as long as the gunner pleases to supply it with ammunition. With the rifle calibre gun, the gunner at his pleasure can fire one shot or any number of shots up to 666 per minute (two belts of 333 cartridges being

MODEL OF THE " MAJESTIC " (BARBETTE).

joined together in the latter case. Although when fired at the rate of 666 per minute the bullets appear to leave the gun in a ceaseless stream, as a matter of fact each bullet departs for its billet with 150 ft. start of its successor. Another interesting fact is that if the bullets were fired aloft at an angle of 45 degrees there would be 400 in the air before the first struck the ground. So perfectly is the gun under control, that Mr. Maxim declares he could write his name with bullets upon a plank in the dark.

Emerging finally into the fresh air, the visitor will no doubt make a point of witnessing the mimic battles on the Lake (a sketch of which forms the frontispiece to this book) and the naval drill in the "arena." The exercises and performances here vary from week to week; for particulars the "Daily Programme" must be consulted. It is well not to leave an Exhibition which is calculated to impress the visitor with a sense of England's naval strength, without a sight of living blue-jackets or naval volunteers. The conditions of naval warfare are altogether changed since "Blake and mighty Nelson fell." But success in the naval wars of the future will still in a large measure depend upon the daring, hardihood, and resourcefulness of the "Mariners of England."

MODEL OF THE "EDINBURGH" (TURRET.)

APPENDIX.

HOW TO GET TO THE EXHIBITION.

I. RAILWAYS. — The Exhibition has, unfortunately, no railway station close to its doors. The nearest is that at Grosvenor Road, which may be recommended to persons living upon the London, Brighton and South Coast, or London, Chatham and Dover systems. The walk from this station to the Exhibition need only take a few minutes. The next nearest railway station is that upon the District Railway at Sloane Square. This is within easy walking distance, and—as will be explained later—there is a good service of 'busses constantly plying between the Square and the Exhibition doors.

II. TRAMS.—Dwellers in the neighbourhood of Battersea and Clapham Junction will find the numerous trams of those districts a convenient means of getting to the Exhibition. Most of these conveyances run to the Surrey side of Chelsea Bridge, at which point a short and pleasant walk is all that remains necessary to bring the visitor to the Hospital grounds at Chelsea. There are plenty of penny omnibuses running to the Exhibition both from Victoria and from Sloane Square station ; and —what is more to our present purpose—there is a special road-car service from the doors every six minutes to and from Liverpool Street via Charing Cross. The fares are—to Victoria Station, a penny ; to Chancery Lane, twopence ; to Liverpool Street threepence. Other 'busses running along the King's Road stop at the top of Smith Street, which is about three minutes walk from the Exhibition.

III. THE RIVER.—Journeying by steamboat is unquestionably the most pleasant mode of reaching Chelsea—especially on a warm summer's day. The Victoria Steamboat Company have erected a pier within a few minutes' walk of the Exhibition, and they run a fairly adequate service of steamers. Steamboats run from London Bridge up the river every twenty minutes or so, and it is probable that further boats will ere long be put on. The journey from Charing Cross pier to the Victoria pier opposite the Exhibition takes a little more than twenty

minutes, and costs twopence. The great drawback to this pleasant mode of travel is that the boats do not run after dusk. The latest homeward-bound boat leaves Chelsea before eight o'clock. There is chance of a later boat coming down the river from Kew, but it is not implicitly to be relied upon.

IV. RAIL AND 'BUS COMBINED.—The orthodox, and in many respects the best, way of getting to the Exhibition is to travel by the District Railway to Sloane Square station, and there to get an omnibus to the door direct. The District Railway is so inextricably bound up with every other Metropolitan and Suburban system, that Sloane Square station may be said to be accessible to almost everybody. From this station omnibuses in the employment of the Company run to and from the Exhibition every twenty minutes ; while other 'busses, the property of the South London Tramway Company, call at Sloane Square in the course of their journey from Knightsbridge to Battersea Bridge, and take up passengers—dropping them, after a short journey, at the Exhibition door. These run every twenty minutes, so that there is a permanent ten minutes' service between Sloane Square station and the Hospital gardens at Chelsea. A pleasant little waiting room has been put up outside the station, and the passengers' comfort is studied in every possible way.

In conclusion, a word as to expense may not be out of place. Of travelling expenses and of refreshments we can say nothing, since these vary with the residence and requirements of the individual. On an ordinary day the Exhibition will cost in " gate-money " alone, if we may use the phrase, half-a-crown. The sum is made up as follows :—

		s.	d.
Entrance to the Exhibition		1	0
" " Lighthouse Model		0	6
" " Trafalgar Panorama		0	6
" " Arctic Scene		0	6
		2	6

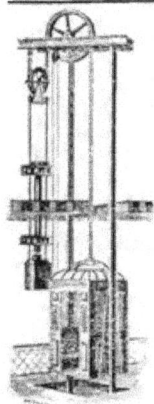

www.ingramcontent.com/pod-product-compliance
Lightning Source LLC
Chambersburg PA
CBHW021513090426
42739CB00007B/599